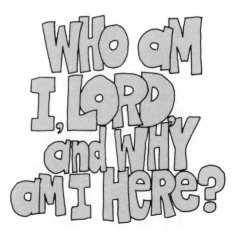

WHO AM I, LORD, and WHY AM I HERE?

Hulme, William & Dale

CONCORDIA

Publishing House
St. Louis

Copyright © 1984 Concordia Publishing House
3558 South Jefferson Avenue
St. Louis, Missouri 63118-3968
Printed in the United States of America

Library of Congress Cataloging in Publication Data

Hulme, William Edward, 1920-
    Who am I, Lord, and why am I here?

    Summary: Discusses, from a Chrstian point of view, the various problems confronting adolescents including peer pressure, drugs, sex, and the appeal of cults and selfish philosophies.
    1. Youth—Religious life. [1. Conduct of life. 2. Christian life] I. Hulme, Dale. II Title. BV4531.2.H84   248.8'3   83-25175
ISBN 0-570-03926-6

---

1   2   3   4   5   6   7   8   9   10   DB   93   92   91   90   89   88   87   86   85   84

Contents

Introduction

(For Adults Only)

*A*lthough this book is primarily for youth, we must acknowledge that adults also will be using it. Remembering that only a child was honest enough to notice that the emperor's new clothes were not, we feel compelled to offer an orientation for those adults.

I remember an incident during my teaching career that greatly influenced my attitude toward young people. I was talking with a student, and we had a little argument over the use of marijuana. She was trying to convince me that marijuana use was not harmful in any way, and I was trying to convince her that it was. The argument went on for several minutes, and soon several students were gathered about, listening and offering their opinions. Finally, in frustration over not being able to resolve this impasse in our relationship, she blurted out, "Mr. Hulme, you don't know what it's like being a teenager now. There are so many pressures on us that weren't on you when you were growing up!"

I was stunned. I thought back over my teen years. There was Vietnam, the draft, the sexual revolution, mind-altering drugs, and much more. It was an era of mind-boggling social upheaval. On the surface, yes, it looks as if my generation had much more to deal with. It seems that the only problem with teenagers these days is their rebelliousness and defiance of traditional values and authority. It often appears that their problems are of their own making. As a result, the message from the adult world is: "No sympathy! Shape up or suffer the consequences!"

But there was something in the earnestness of her face, in the desperation of her expression. She made me think. Could it be that there is something in the fabric of our contemporary society that makes life more difficult for teenagers?

The answer I arrived at is: Yes, there are things that could make life more difficult for teenagers today, but life does not *have* to be more difficult for them. The teen years are naturally a time of

7

tremendous change, excitement, and anxiety. They are years of intense feelings. They are years of puberty, adolescence, and maturation. And for some they are years of intense isolation.

My student's expression of frustration was in large part only a timeless expression of the teenage heart—an expression of isolation, of being cut off from the adult world. Adults all too quickly forget what it was like being a teenager, and one of the greatest pressures on teenagers is to become something they are not—to grow up faster than they want or are able to.

In this book we will look at and discuss some of the problems teenagers encounter in their teen years. If we were to isolate one single factor that unifies these concerns, it would be identity formation. It is in the teen years that a person develops from a dependent to an independent identity.

We will look at the concerns of identity formation from a synthesis standpoint—from both the experience of teenagers (most of the material in this book was derived from actual experiences of teenagers), and from the vantage point of adulthood—the vantage point of being able to look back at the whole process of identity formation. We look back perhaps with a sigh of relief, but a wistful one at that. Even if we cannot relive our own youth, we can't imagine a world without the joy, excitement, and meaning that young people impart to our lives.

But what is the monster lurking in the fabric of our contemporary culture that makes life more difficult for teenagers today? I remember when it hit the schools. One year there were plenty of longhairs still running around the halls with painted faces, Afros, beads, and bells; there were student rights, pacifism, expanded consciousness, earnestness, awareness, and kids too old for their age. The next year they were all gone. Everyone was into getting good grades. Teacher reactions ranged from astonishment to bored omniscience—"I knew it would all eventually pass."

But there was something else going on, something that had already occurred in our society at large. One student expressed it well: "I guess there's not much left to do but get good grades and get high." That seems like a strange combination, but it is a true representation of teenage priorities. If you ask any representative group of teenagers today what is most important to them, you will find good grades and parties ranking in the top. It's not that parties are bad (I enjoy the fellowship of parties, too!) or that all youth will give these answers (Some young people don't like partying, but is that altogether good?), but the trend is evident throughout our whole society.

It is as if we cast aside all wisdom and maturity in the 1960s and opened all the doors to the rooms where the monsters had been caged. It's no wonder they were so fascinating; they had been imprisoned for so long that we didn't know why they were chained up anymore. Having access to all the rooms was great excitement for a while, but it was finally revealed to be unrealistic, idealistic.

The message that then quickly moved throughout America was "Back to the basics. Back to reality—good grades, career, and status." But something had changed. A monster had been loosed, and there wasn't any way to get it back into its dungeon. "Good grades and getting high." The monster is self-indulgence—instant gratification.

We have become a "Society on the Take."* The result is a double standard. Youth are asked to abide by the old back-to-the-basics values but are bombarded with encouragement and incentives to instantly gratify themselves. The youth market (whether consumed by teenagers or others) has become a very important sector of our economy. No wonder there is such political pressure to provide jobs for teenagers! Our economy would be shaken without their contribution to the gross national product. As primary consumers, teenagers are expected to make important decisions about their lives, decisions that often involve value conflicts. The result is enormous pressure on teens. Teenage suicide, homicide, drug use, pregnancy, venereal disease, vandalism, and crime are all increasing, all as direct results of this pressure. And the isolation is ever increasing, too.

Teenagers are more and more alone in their situation. Adults cannot understand it because it has all changed so fast. Teenagers trust adults less now than ever. Father no longer knows best in the popular culture. News of some real scary results is starting to trickle in. Young people are not reporting rapes, burglaries, robberies, and even murders because they do not trust or believe in the values of the adult generation. When a whole high school in California can know about the murder of a classmate and not say anything, there is an enormous problem.

But life does not *have* to be more difficult for teenagers today.

---

* Howard G. Garner, "Children of the 'Society on the Take,' " *Christian Century*, XCV, 35 (Nov. 1, 1978), 1044-1048.

Pandora's box may have been opened, but this time hope was not locked in when the box was closed. Hope was let out of the box long before the present social situation began. That hope has endured many trials over the years that would make the present situation look like child's play. The hope that God placed into the world when He gave His Son for us was permanent. Although the present situation may look pretty dismal for teens—particularly those in inner city environments, the poor, and the minorities—there is still hope. There is the hope of Jesus Christ for a new life—for redemption. There is always the possibility of a fresh start.

In this book we will discuss several issues of concern to teens in contemporary American society. Some will be concerns naturally occurring in all teenagers, such as the concerns of identity formation. Others will be particularly associated with the contemporary American society such as drug use, teen pregnancy, and suicide. We will look at all of them in the light of the Gospel, with the Good News of redemption offering the possibility of starting over. We will follow a format of story, discussion, and exercise. The exercises will be of value whether you are reading this book as part of a group activity, or as an individual.

There is so much written these days that I wonder if one more book will do any good. It will if we get at the guts of the issues and if we write in the name of Him to whom our future has been entrusted. That is the challenge of this book, and it is the challenge that we have attempted to meet. We hope you appreciate the sincerity with which we approached the task, but we also hope you appreciate the lightheartedness. There is joy and a good amount of fun to be had if we can step aside from ourselves and look with humor on the whole process. So don't take it as an insult if you, teenager, happened to have read this "forbidden" chapter. The most convenient part of a book to skip is the introduction, and we wanted to make sure you read it. We knew you would.

1

My Body

*T*he turning point for Lisa came during her first junior high gym class. Perhaps she had been protected before, but now the eyes of her peers were on her. Some glanced and looked away. Others looked for a while and then averted their glance. Some just stared. Fortunately, the girls didn't ridicule her. Most of the barbs and jeers were directed toward other girls—fat girls, flat-chested girls, or girls who had not yet developed. Why is it, Lisa thought, that some girls are so ashamed of their bodies, and others are so conceited? It was then that Lisa realized that in order to be somebody in this world, she would have to improve her physical self-image. She tried out for soccer, floor hockey, and track. For the next six years she played one or all of these sports, developing her strength and skill until she became a respected athlete at her school. With success in sports came popularity, and Lisa had fun in high school. She felt good about herself. What Lisa really considers important about her decision to go out for sports is that she refused to be put down by her body. It was very tempting to hide her body and withdraw from the scene. Some girls did. All that was needed to get out of gym was a doctor's excuse. But Lisa was a fighter. Some of the other girls were caught by surprise at that first gym class. It was the first time their bodies had been subjected to the scrutiny of their peers. But Lisa was prepared. She had long before become resigned to her body. It was at that class that she decided to love it.

Being Wholly Yourself

*C*an you separate the way you feel about yourself from the way you feel about your body? That is, can you feel good about yourself if you are ashamed of your body for some reason or other? What about your mind? Can you feel good about yourself if you are ashamed of your intelligence? Maybe you don't think much about your spirit, but can you feel good about yourself if you are ashamed of your spirituality?

Body, mind, and spirit—these are the three components of your self, and who you are has to do with how you feel about each of these. How can you be yourself if you are either ashamed or conceited about any of these? If you are constantly trying to hide some aspect of yourself, or if you are trying to be phony about who you are, how can you be yourself? On the flip side, are you really being yourself if you are overly conceited about any of these? Often someone who is conceited about body, mind, or spirituality is trying to compensate for something that is felt to be lacking in another area.

"Being myself" is important, but, as you well know, it is also difficult. It is helpful to recognize the components of the self—body, mind, and spirit. (Some people add "feelings" to these three. Also, "spirit" and "soul" can sometimes be interchanged.) To be yourself, you have to be true to your body, true to your mind, and true to your soul. In medicine this approach is called "wholistic." Wholistic medicine maintains that good health involves the interplay of the three components of the self. If one of these is not doing well, the others are affected. For instance, if someone is suffering from a physical ailment such as frequent headaches, the doctor might see if there is some mental or psychosomatic cause, such as stress. Some spiritual malaise could also be contributing to the headaches. If someone has mental problems—for example, depression—physical exercise might help. "Spiritual exercise" might also be useful. (Spiritual can mean more than just worship. Prayer is also a spiritual activity. Visiting someone in need could be, too.)

When I was a teenager, I could find very little in the Bible that related to my needs and concerns. Part of the problem was that I was not very observant and part was that the Bible is very challenging reading material. The Bible deals directly with the issue of "being oneself," and it gives it a twist you will find nowhere else. The words *whole, holy,* and *righteous* all have about the same meaning. Being oneself or being whole has to do with being *holy.* The word *holy* often conjures up images of very religious individuals who are always perfect with halos hovering about their heads.

But the word does not allow for spiritual conceit. The Bible gives it a remarkably different twist. The Good News of the Gospel tells us that being holy does not mean that you are better than others. Nor does it mean that you have to become better than others to be called holy. The Gospel tells us that the one and only thing we need to be holy is faith in Jesus Christ. In other words, believing in Jesus is absolutely essential to being yourself.

For a teenager, being oneself is particularly difficult because the self is in continual and colossal change. Just when you think you have finally matured, you have a growth spurt. Just when you finally get comfortable with your appearance, you develop the worst case of pimples you ever had. The changes of the body are the most obvious. You enter the teen years in the body of a child, and you exit with that of an adult. It is easy to observe the changes and describe them—maturation of the sexual organs, increased body hair, development of secondary sexual characteristics, etc. What we don't often think of is that these changes are taking you somewhere. These changes are programmed by God for wholeness. We were created to be perfect—holy—and that is the direction that all of these changes are taking you. The changes in the body are good. It is just difficult keeping up with them and feeling comfortable—that is, neither ashamed nor conceited—with them.

When you are a child, you really don't have an independent self. That is, whoever you are as a child cannot stand alone in this world and survive. That is all part of the program, too. While you are a teenager, you are becoming "somebody." You are not becoming a carbon copy of your parents, and you are not becoming a replica or a clone. You are becoming an individual. You will be unique, and the most obvious uniqueness is your body. The current "punk" movement is an attempt to prove uniqueness. The idea behind "punk" is to be different by appearance—to affirm the uniqueness of the self in the face of everything in our society that tends to homogenize and stereotype us. If you think about it, the movement is unnecessary. Are there any two bodies alike?

Accepting Our Bodies

A lot of teenagers are embarrassed about their bodies. Considering what the pressure is in matching up with the opposite sex, it is no wonder there is a lot of anxiety about appearance. When I was a teenager, I had trouble accepting my body because I was small and cute rather than tall, well-built, and handsome. I always felt inferior, and that was not all bad because I compensated by getting into sports and body-building—activities that I enjoy very much as an adult and that I might not have gotten involved in had I not had trouble accepting my body.

This problem of not accepting my body stayed with me until a significant event occurred during my first year at college. I worked out with a wrist developer. One day my roommate, a tall, well-built, and handsome football hero, came in and watched me work out. Embarrassed, I put down the developer. My roommate started to chuckle. I felt more embarrassed. His wrists were easily twice the size of mine, but he shouldn't have laughed. He shouldn't have been conceited about what he had been given.

"You have skinny wrists," he said. I almost melted. He had said it. He knew what I was trying to hide. The skinny wrists were just the tip of the iceberg. It was my whole self-concept. I felt inferior all over, and he must have known it. But he was really a gentle and understanding person. He said, "There was a time when I would have made a deal with God to have a body like yours—skinny wrists and all. But I've accepted my body. I suppose I had to accept it earlier, because it was brought to my attention as a child, when you were normal."

I looked at his tall, well-built, and handsome body, wondering what he was talking about. Why did he call me "normal"? What did he have to "accept" about his body? Then it dawned on me. There it was, etched across his face like a ditch—invisible to me now because I knew him so well. My roommate had a harelip, and the scar was deep and wide across his face. It was then that I decided to accept my body and be myself. I realized that I was programmed, not to be tall, well-built, and handsome, but to be uniquely me, and I accepted that.

I Holy and Not Holy at the Same Time

t says in the Bible that we were made male and female and in the image of God (Gen. 1:26). There is considerable difficulty in understanding what the image of God really means because no one has ever seen God (John 1:18), and it is difficult to imagine the great, mighty, omnipotent God walking about in a human body like George Burns in the movie *Oh, God*. But in some way being created in the image of God must mean that we are designed to be whole, to be right, to be holy. However, though we were designed to be whole, right, and holy, we are not, and when people think they are, we correctly think they are conceited, arrogant, or just plain phonies (hypocrites). Something has happened. We are *not* whole, righteous, or holy. There are things we do that rob us of wholeness. Yet we have the *promise* that we are programmed for wholeness. We are on a journey, a journey that lasts a lifetime, a journey that follows a program toward wholeness.

God in a Body

Now do you see why it is so difficult to "be oneself"? It means we have to accept ourselves in an imperfect condition, and that is not easy to do. Actually, if you can accept someone even with their imperfections, then you must really love them. So to accept yourself, you have to love yourself, and that includes loving your body.

Do you love your body? Think of how we would take care of our bodies if we really loved them. We wouldn't smoke, eat junk food, or get venereal disease. We would exercise, sleep well, and eat the right foods. We can all discover some way we do not live up to love.

We know that God loves our bodies even though we don't live up to His image. How do we know that? Isn't it our bodies—their appetites and desires, their lusts and self-love—that get us into all the trouble, that keep us from being whole, from being acceptable? Teenagers have rebelled against this put-down of the body since time immemorial and with good reason. It is not only our bodies that cause the trouble. It is our minds and souls also. Why single out the body and pick on it? God loves our bodies, and we should too. We know God loves our bodies because He came to us in the flesh—in a real body. It wasn't a body that disappeared every time the situation got a little too hot to handle. It wasn't a body that avoided all of the teenage changes that you are going through. The purpose of Jesus' life in the body was to show us that God did indeed love us and to show us a way for us to be restored to wholeness. Then Jesus died to take away our sins that prevent us from becoming whole—the sins that prevent us from completing our program.

It is hard for us to think about sin because we have to admit we are doing something wrong. It is even harder for us to think about taking away sins. How can you reverse something that has already been done? It takes a miracle—the miracle of forgiveness! When we are forgiven by the blood of Jesus Christ, our sins are taken away and we are whole. As baptized Christians, we have this forgiveness every moment of our lives. It is like a new life within the old, and that is a good thing for our whole being, body, mind, and soul.

As Christians, we have a lot of work to do in this world, and we need strong, healthy bodies to do it. Everywhere we go in the world, we will have to confront obstacles to God's love, and that may take a lot of strength.

I'm glad I had the opportunity to meet Lisa, and I'm thankful for the opportunity to pass along to you what I learned from her. The lesson she taught me was that even if my body is not perfect, and even if I do not take care of it like I should, I can always start over and love it. If Lisa could learn to love her body as she did on that first day in junior high physical education, then I guess I can love mine. Lisa was born with cerebral palsy. Her body is twisted and misshapen. It doesn't always do what she wants it to. Sometimes it moves when she doesn't want it to, and sometimes it doesn't move when she wants it to. But during that first day at junior high physical education she learned to love it, twisted and misshapen as it was. She participated in sports in a wheelchair. If she can love her body, I guess I can love mine, and you can love yours, too.

*T*HINGS YOU CAN DO

Individual: For a one-week period, try one physical activity for one hour each day. Evaluate at the end of the week. How do you feel? You might also try to avoid sweets for a whole week. Try to abstain from cigarettes for a week if you are a smoker. Evaluate. You will never know if you can feel better about your body unless you try some of these things. The following is a quiz that will assist you in evaluating your care for your body.

Health Care Quiz

A	B	
yes	no	1. Did you eat more than three sweets per day for the past week? Include jelly, pop, candy, cakes, cookies, donuts, pancake syrup, etc.
yes	no	2. Did you eat more than three saturated fats per day for the past week? A saturated fat is one that is solid or comes from meat products. Examples are meat fat, homogenized milk, ice cream, cheese, coconut oil, lard, bacon, sausage, butter, etc.
no	yes	3. Did you eat foods every day from each of the four

food groups (dairy products, fruits and vegetables, meat and fish, grains—preferably whole)?

no   yes   4. Did you do some form of exercise this past week for at least a half hour per day?

yes   no   5. Did you drink more than one cup of coffee (or two cokes or one and one half cups of tea) each day this past week?

yes   no   6. Did you smoke cigarettes this past week?

yes   no   7. Do you live in an industrial community?

yes   no   8. Did you use any mood-altering drugs this past week?

no   yes   9. Did you sleep at least seven hours a day every day this past week?

no   yes 10. Did you brush your teeth and floss every day this past week?

Tabulate the B column, giving one point for each question. Score: 9—10 EXCELLENT; 7—8 VERY GOOD; 5—6 GOOD; 3—4 FAIR; 0—2 POOR.

Group: Your group at church is a place where you can talk about meaningful things with others who will share a Christian approach. The best activity your group could pursue regarding your approach to your body is to invite a handicapped person or persons to speak to the group. Peers would be best. Some type of interaction, particularly sports, with handicapped persons would be ideal. Have the speakers read chapter one and react to it.

If it is not possible to get a handicapped person to speak, follow a format of introduction, roleplaying, and discussion. Introduction questions: Do you have a physical handicap? Are there physically handicapped people in your group? Do you know anyone with a physical handicap? What do you think it would be like to be handicapped? Do you ever feel that there is something wrong with your body?

Roleplaying: If you have not done roleplaying in a group before, please refer to the description of roleplaying in the appendix. Have the group break into pairs and move into separate areas. Have each person take a turn at roleplaying a handicapped student who has just entered your school. The other person plays himself/herself. After five minutes ask the participants to switch roles. After 10 minutes return to the group.

Group discussion: Which role was more awkward? What kinds of things did you say to introduce yourself and welcome the handicapped person into your school? Did either role make you think about your own body? Is there any way in which you are handicapped? Do you accept your body? Do you love your body?

2

Feelings and Forgiveness

An "Odd Couple"

*E*arl and Gary are friends although it is difficult to understand why. They seem so different. Earl is considered a "good" boy. Yet he often seems emotionally flat and is frequently bored. He has a strong need to please his parents to keep him from feeling rejected. One day he ran into trouble with his mother. He became a temporary scapegoat for her anger. She resented her employer but could not express this to her. Instead she took it out on Earl. Earl couldn't understand what was going on. He was devastated by her "dumping" on him.

In his depression Earl went to his pastor, and together they looked into what was happening to him when his mother attacked him. He felt rejected by her. He didn't realize that parents have troubles of their own that can come out indirectly.

Gary, on the other hand, is considered "fun loving." Yet his "fun" is largely focused on sensual pleasure. He has a strong need for excitement to keep him from thinking about himself. One day Gary heard a very moving address on sexual responsibility at his church youth group. Some of the things he heard pricked his conscience, and he felt guilty over the way he had been treating girls.

Gary wasn't one to talk with anybody. Finally he had to talk to somebody, and he chose Earl. While Earl lacked the counseling skills and experience of the pastor, he was a good listener. Gary began to realize that he secretly envied Earl because he seemed to have it all together. Earl on the other hand saw that he had been envying Gary for all the fun he was having. In talking together each discovered that what the other envied was only skin deep.

Gary and Earl were more alike than they realized. Both were

afraid of their feelings. Both had an identity problem, and each in his own way was trying to prove something. Both were running from their uneasy feelings about themselves.

Gary was afraid of boredom and needed excitement. But why fear boredom? He didn't like his own company because the pieces of his life didn't fit together. Boredom brought this unpleasant reality to his mind.

Earl was afraid of being rejected by his parents. But why fear rejection? Because of the loneliness it brings with it. He was trying to be the model son by conforming to the image of a "good" boy.

A Quest for Good Feelings

You may recognize something of yourself in either or both of these boys. Who has not run from uncomfortable feelings? At the same time, who has not desired good feelings? God has designed us to have not only thoughts but feelings, and sometimes we do not seem to have much control over either. Have you noticed how your thoughts affect how you feel and how your feelings affect how you think?

Take your good feelings, for example. When you feel affectionate toward someone or are enthusiastic about something, you feel excited and your body seems to tingle. When you have these good feelings, you find yourself thinking good thoughts as well.

Now take your bad feelings. They are not bad in the sense of being evil but bad in that they make you feel bad. For example, how did you feel when you didn't have a date for the school dance, or when you got a bad grade, or didn't make it in the "try-outs"? Sad? Mad? Bummed out? Depressed? Scared? When you have such feelings, don't your thoughts seem to match them?

Good and bad feelings go with being human. If you want to have only good feelings, you are pursuing an illusion. Our feelings change a lot—sometimes even the same day or the same hour. They are like a roller coaster—always moving up and down.

If we try to escape from our uncomfortable feelings, we may also lose out on good feelings. Earl's emotional flatness was due to his fear of painful feelings. He protected himself from them by not feeling much of anything. Actually he had deep feelings, but he didn't let himself know it.

Gary protected himself from his feelings by not getting involved seriously with anything or anyone. When we put ourselves into something, we *feel* one way or another. Gary's pursuit of sensual pleasure involved his body but not his person. This is what got to him—he realized he was *using* girls, not *caring* for them. By remaining inwardly detached, he was trying to avoid being hurt.

Earl's conformity was also only a form behind which he hid his real self. He didn't put himself into things either, and for the same reason. Neither boy risked showing his real self to others.

Getting involved—putting oneself into what one is doing—is risky. Because we are exposed, we are vulnerable, and because we are vulnerable, we can get hurt. When we put ourselves into what we are doing, there is little protection from our feelings. They come on strong. Now what do we do with them? Our feelings need to be educated just like our intellects. Although feelings can be painful, it is by facing our pains that we grow. They are really "growing pains."

*O*ur faith in God helps us to deal with our painful feelings. We

You Are in Control—Under God

Our faith in God helps us to deal with our painful feelings. We believe He is with us even though our pains seem to deny His presence. Believing in Jesus also means getting involved because believing means trusting. If we are afraid to risk, we are afraid to trust. Instead we limit ourselves to what we can control. Gary was trying to control things so that he wouldn't get bored. Earl was trying to control things so that he wouldn't be rejected. Both were trying to avoid being hurt.

To believe in Jesus means to trust Him to take care of us. Then we can let go of our need to control. It is when we trust in Him that He reveals Himself to us. We get to know him better and in particular to know that He is trustworthy.

There is a difference between trusting in God and tempting Him. We are also to use the good sense He has given us. Risking does not mean acting recklessly and irrationally. Rather it means that we can enter into opportunities that we are not sure we can control because we are trusting Him to take care of us. The fear is that He may not take care of us in the way we had in mind.

We feel trapped by our troublesome feelings, and this adds to our fear of them. They seem to be controlling us rather than we controlling them. This can be scary, particularly since these feelings are so painful. Take moods for example. You don't decide to get into a mood; it just seems to descend on you. It also threatens to stay with you.

21

Actually we have more control over our feelings than we think. For instance, when you sense the mood coming on, you can either withdraw from others and become quiet, or you can seek out company and talk. You are more likely to disperse the mood if you seek out company and talk. While it is hard to converse when you are down, it is not impossible, and it is the most direct way out of your mood.

To be in control of yourself depends on your feeling good about yourself. Otherwise you may get too down on yourself to care. In spite of the misgivings you may have about yourself, God forgives you for everything. He really does! In Jesus He became one of us to do for us what we could not do for ourselves. Through Jesus' life, death, and resurrection He has removed every barrier that could separate you from Him. In your baptism you received this gift of forgiveness. Therefore you can say with St. Paul, "If God is for us, who is against us?" (Rom. 8:31). For this is what the cross of Christ means—God is *for* you!

God is reaching out through the cross to embrace you—all parts of you. Through the cross He is saying, "You are My child. See how much I love you. See how much I care." Here is a love that has no conditions attached to it; so receive what He wants to give you. You will realize how good it feels to be loved, to be embraced, by God. Every day, every hour, can be a renewal of your baptism.

Y Freed by Forgiveness

our feelings are forgiven because *you* are forgiven. Yet your feelings in themselves are not your sins—not even your bad feelings. Your feelings are simply a barometer of what is going on in your life. "How do you feel about it?" is a "right-on" question. Answering it helps you know yourself. Once you know what is going on in your life, you can decide what to do about it.

First you decide what to do about your feelings. While your feelings themselves are not sinful, they can lead you into sin if you do not deal with them wisely. Take anger, for example. There is nothing wrong in itself with feeling angry. God is capable of anger, and because we are made in His image we are also. But St. Paul warns us, "Be angry but do not sin; do not let the sun go down on your anger" (Eph. 4:26). If we ignore our anger or go to the opposite extreme and fan it into a flame, we can turn it into attitudes of resentment and hostility. Such attitudes distort the way we think; they are sinful.

Another bad feeling is sadness. In our day we call it depression or being bummed out. It was once called melancholia. Feeling sad is part of our humanity, and it is not necessarily of our sinful humanity. There is a lot in this world to feel sad about. However, if we ignore our sad feelings or go to the opposite extreme and nurse them, they can develop into pessimistic and cynical attitudes. Because they undermine our hope and trust, such attitudes are sinful.

So accept your feelings as part of the humanity that God has given you. When you are aware of your feelings, express them to yourself and to God: "I feel angry, or sad, or guilty, or scared, or flat, or elated, or excited." You are loved in the midst of your feelings even though some of them make you feel unlovable. When you are able to tell God how you feel, regardless of the feelings, you obviously believe that He can accept you as you are.

If this is the case, then you also can accept yourself, including your feelings. Once you can accept your feelings, you can understand better what is going on inside of you. Then you can be in control of yourself. You can live positively with your humanity, even your sinful humanity. The bad things in your past lose their power to influence your present. You are free!

Freedom to Learn and to Change

*W*hat Earl and Gary need to do is to risk feeling their feelings. Gary's fear of boredom is really fear of despair, but Gary isn't going to know this until he allows himself to *feel* his fear. He needs to face the emptiness behind his apparent fun. That emptiness needs to be filled so that his life will have purpose and meaning.

The forgiveness we receive through Jesus gives us the power to change. It makes it possible for us to learn from experience. When we have a humiliating or otherwise painful experience, we don't even like to think about it, let alone learn from it. Instead of profiting from such experiences we repeat them. Our life then goes in circles— meaningless circles.

This is what dawned on both Earl and Gary as they saw what was happening in their lives. Both were repeating the same old self-defeating behaviors. They realized that God's forgiveness made it possible for them to do something else. Their past was one thing, but their present and future were something else. Through forgiveness they could learn from their past failures rather than repeat them.

Gary and Earl are moving now and in the right direction. They may have their times of regression when their bad feelings get the best of them. But they will know what to do if this should happen. They will confess to God; He will forgive them, and they will start over once again.

When you go to the Lord's Supper at your next opportunity, do as Jesus said to do—do it in remembrance of Him. As you receive His body and blood through the bread and wine, remind yourself that it is through His broken body on the cross and His shed blood that you are forgiven. As you take the elements into your body, "see" this forgiveness going into every part of *you*—into every memory and every hurt and every guilt. Holy Communion is God's way of giving you the reassurance you need that you are loved as you are. It is a way He has chosen for you to renew your baptismal covenant.

No wonder this Sacrament is also called the Eucharist, which means the Thanksgiving. You are forgiven—thoroughly, completely, wholly, fully, freely, and forever. Praise the Lord!

*T*HINGS YOU CAN DO

Individual: There are things you can do to teach yourself to live positively with your feelings. The first is to become aware of them—to *feel* them. The second is to acknowledge and accept them. The third is to direct them in healthy ways. Because you live in God's covenant of forgiveness, you can do all three.

A practical way to carry out this education in feelings is to keep a journal in which you can record your awareness of your feelings and how you feel about them. A journal is not the same as a diary. You would not need to record in it on a daily basis for example. Rather, when you have a significant awareness of feelings, good or bad, write a description of this experience, emphasizing how you felt—or are still feeling. Do this in a prayerful way, being aware of God's forgiving presence as you think about the experience. If you are still feeling the feelings, you can practice right then telling God how you feel.

Besides writing your feeling experiences in a journal and sharing your feelings with God in prayer, you can also share at least some of these feeling experiences with a trusted friend—your parents, the pastor or other adult counselors at church or school, or a peer.

There is always a risk in such sharing that your trusted confidant won't be as good a listener or as trustworthy as you thought. But there is an even greater risk if you don't share. You need sharing relationships for your personal growth.

Group: Your youth group at church is another practical means through which you can learn to live positively with your feelings. There must be accepted ground rules before your group can be a sharing group, however, and the foremost of these is confidentiality. Review the ground rules in the appendix for group interaction, especially those regarding confidentiality.

Besides the support you get from sharing your feeling experiences with the group, you can also dramatize a particularly difficult situation in order to get additional help. You need a competent leader to direct this sort of activity. You would follow the same format of introduction, roleplay, and discussion as described in the previous chapter. Let's say you are having a difficult time with a particular teacher. You can tell the group about a situation with this teacher in which you need help. Somebody in the group can take the role of the teacher, using a fictitious name, of course. You can take your own role and interact with the "teacher" in the roleplay. Then both of you can share with the group the feelings you experience during the roleplay. Do it again, but reverse the roles; you take the role of the teacher. Both of you should again share your feelings with the group. In this way you will learn to feel also with your "adversary." You will discover that you are much better prepared to deal with the real-life situation with your teacher.

3

Friends and Popularity

Daniel

*T*here were several groups of students in the school Daniel went to, and you could identify with whatever group you chose. There were, of course, jocks and preppies. There were roguish groups and cool groups like the "punkers." The problem, however, was that the group you might choose to be in might not accept you.

When Daniel entered Kennedy High School, he decided that he would like to be in the most popular group. Like the other young people in the popular group, Daniel got good grades, was involved in sports, and participated in extracurricular activities. His first disappointment came when one of the students in the group told him, "Daniel, I know you would like to come to my party Saturday night, but I can't really invite you. You aren't really in our group. Do you understand? I hope you do."

So Daniel tried another route. He knew that if he went with one of the girls in the popular group, he could at least go to the parties. Once there, he would be able to impress them with his hipness or coolness or whatever it would take. So Daniel waited until one of the girls in the most popular group was available and then, summoning all his courage, he asked her out. It worked! Well, it wasn't easy. The girl, Karen, was spoiled and gave him a terrible and humiliating initiation. The first thing she said to him when he got in the car was, "Wow! You're a lot shorter than I thought you were!" After Daniel fielded that one, things got a little better, and she asked him to a party the next week.

At the party Daniel made sure he made an impression. Unfortunately, he made the impression that he didn't belong in their group. Rather, it looked like he belonged in a more roguish group. Daniel got roaring drunk and rowdy. He even accidently broke the toilet seat. He didn't drink any more than the other people at the party, but Daniel really hadn't drunk much before because of his athletic commitments. He couldn't hold his liquor very well. After the first drink he felt a little less uptight. So he had another. Then he was feeling downright buzzed. He started talking loudly and making a show—more drinks and more of a show. Pretty soon the toilet seat was broken, and the host asked him to leave.

Not only did Daniel get in trouble at the host's house, but he also got in trouble when he got home. He thought he was sneaking into the house, but he stumbled so badly over everything that he woke his parents. "I'm just making my way to the bedroom," he said with a silly grin on his face. Not only did he get grounded for two weeks, but he got unceremoniously removed from the popular group. The next day one of his "friends" in the popular group called and said, "Daniel, sit down. I have bad news for you. Karen is going with Eddy."

That didn't take long, thought Daniel. The next call was from the host of the party. He informed Daniel that they didn't really want him hanging around them anymore because he had a bad image. The final humiliation was on the bus. Karen approached him and said in a loud voice, "I suppose you think that shirt is attractive. Well, gag me with a spoon! You wouldn't catch Eddy wearing trash like that."

It was over. The hurt was almost unbearable, and Daniel, though he didn't think of suicide, didn't ever want to go back to Kennedy High School for the rest of his life. In fact, he didn't go to school for a week, but his mother finally sent him to a doctor who pronounced him fit to go to school.

So Daniel went back, and now he looked for the people who disliked the popular group. Their type was considered roguish; most of the guys in it used drugs and committed vandalism. It flew in the face of all of Daniel's values to use drugs, but it seemed he was on an express train, and there was no getting off until he got justice! So Daniel got into the group. At first it was uncomfortable doing some of the things that he had been taught not to do. This group was *bad!* They were into drugs and sex and crime. If you drank enough or got high enough, you could even enjoy it. In fact, it was exciting!

It didn't take long however, to run into heat from his parents. The first time Daniel stayed out all night, he heard it—grounded.

Well, it didn't take Daniel long to figure out that being grounded is good only as long as you put up with it. So he just walked out the door—right in front of his parents. "Too bad," he said, "I ain't coming back."

I didn't see Daniel for several years. I had known him when I was a teacher at Kennedy High. When he dropped out of high school, I didn't think much of it and soon forgot about him. He was like so many others—nice kids but always in trouble or high. They eventually drop out.

Then one day six years later I met Daniel again. I was doing an internship in a halfway house for criminal offenders. Daniel was one of the young men there. He didn't recognize me, and I must admit I didn't really recognize him. He looked white, too white to be healthy, as though he never got outside. Tattoos marred his arms—crude homemade types and professional ones. He wore a T-shirt, a plain, dirty white T-shirt, and ragged blue jeans.

"Daniel," I said, "you look like someone I knew once. Can you tell me a little about yourself?"

"Aw, there ain't much to tell," he replied. "I ain't much. I ain't done nothing all my life. I'm more or less a bum, as you can see. What do you want to know?"

I asked him about his parents.

"Oh, I guess I pretty much let them down," he replied. "I left home in high school. At first my parents kept dragging me back. They'd send the cops after me, and they finally sent me to juvenile for running away. I sat it out, and when I got out, I ran away for good. That's when I got into dealing. I guess my folks just gave up on me because I used to deal right here in the city, even at Kennedy. They must have seen me sometime. But I didn't know it would end up like this. It was all so much fun for a while."

I knew Daniel seemed so much more defeated than some of the other inmates, so I asked him about it.

"Well, don't tell them I told you this," Daniel said. "They're still using. I'm trying to change. I go to AA, and there you got to admit all the things you done wrong . . . did wrong. See, I really messed up my life. I can't even talk right anymore."

I went home that night with a lump in my throat. How could anyone lose so much? I could not believe that anyone could have such a low opinion of himself, especially someone like Daniel who had been so concerned about being popular. I didn't know if I wanted to visit with him anymore. He just seemed to have too many

28

problems for me to get involved with. But I kept getting this image of him at night. I could go home and do whatever I wanted. I could read a good book, see a movie, visit a friend, or whatever. But Daniel probably wouldn't do anything except go to bed. I could picture him lying in his bed at night, all alone, and thinking about his life. How could God let any kid end up like that? But I knew he was right. The other guys were still using. That's why they were so cheery and high all the time. At least Daniel was on the road home. I hoped he realized that he would need a lot of patience. The road back is long and hard.

WPopularity and Peer Pressure

hat is there about popularity that will make young people sacrifice so much to attain it? This is probably one of the things about being a teenager that adults have the most difficult time remembering. Adults can't remember the pressure of popularity because it is a grim reminder of the pressure of conformity that still rules their lives. I am confiding this fact to you (as a teenager) so you know this is not a problem unique to adolescence. It is a rare person, teen or adult, who can withstand the pressures of popularity or conformity and just be themselves. Adults laugh at teenagers who primp in front of the mirror or who have to have just the right clothes, but adults rarely wear clothing that makes them look different either. It is the rare person who can resist peer pressure.

The importance of being true to yourself, of being genuine, authentic, or just "yourself," has been brought up before in this book. There is probably no more powerful enemy to being yourself than "peer pressure." Peer pressure is the pressure that people your own age (peers) put on you to be accepted or popular. Peer pressure works on you from the inside because you want to be accepted. You don't want to be inferior, inadequate, or different. So you respond to whatever will make you accepted or popular. I don't have to tell you that sometimes, as for Daniel, these demands go against your values. That is when peer pressure heats you up to exploding!

Some people, you might think, never feel the anxiety of peer pressure. They so obviously cannot meet the demands of acceptability that they are identified and labeled as "out of it" or "nobody" from the very start. Unfortunately, the power of peer pressure is so strong that such judgment is a curse for most of these "nobodies." It is hard to stand up for yourself and say, "Well, I just don't care if I am popular. I'm just going to be myself!" Most extremely unpopular people suffer from peer pressure, too, but they feel anguish rather than anxiety. If you have the heart, you might want to befriend some of the "nobodies" in your school. You might find they have a lot in common with you. You might find that they, like you, are basically shy. If you consider yourself to be a "nobody," take heart. Often the less popular people in high school become more successful later and enjoy adult life more because they have had to struggle with the pains of being true to themselves earlier in life. Jesus said, "The last will be first, and the first [will be] last" (Matt. 20:16). And He wasn't just talking about the way it is in heaven!

People like Daniel are in the zone between knowing for sure they are acceptable to their peers and knowing for sure they are not. This is the most dangerous position because it is tempting to compromise your values in order to be accepted or popular. If you feel this is your situation and you feel the anxiety of peer pressure, be careful. Being popular does not necessarily mean that you are somebody.

I remember when a friend of mine died in high school. I was driving home from the hospital and picked up a classmate hitchhiking. He was a young person, like Daniel, who was trying very hard to be popular. When I told him about the death, his response was "Well, he was nobody anyway." Right then I knew that, even though he was dead, my friend was more a "somebody" than this "nobody" I had picked up! But I felt ashamed for this hitchhiker. Deep down inside he had a conscience. He wasn't being true to himself. He was following the demand of peer pressure. Although the hitchhiker and Daniel may be extreme cases, we all sacrifice our values in some way to the demands of peer pressure. If we know this, why do we let it happen?

I The Power of Peer Pressure

t is almost impossible to go through life all alone. We all have to find some group of people in which we can be accepted. Even one close friend can sometimes be enough, but, if you don't have another person or persons to fall back on, the loneliness and shame of rejection may seem too much to bear. Then you may be tempted to compromise your values rather than be isolated by rejection. Parents can help by supporting you, but they don't always provide the approval you desire. Ultimately you will separate from your family and have to find your support and approval elsewhere. That is one of the reasons peer pressure is so strong. You know that ultimately it is among your peers that you must find your place in life.

Adults, too, face peer pressure and the temptation to sacrifice their values to the demands of conformity. The difference, however, is that for teenagers the compromise can be deadly in the short run rather than the long run. Although as a teenager you are sharp for the short run, you lack experience and are vulnerable to the pitfalls and hazards of life. You know some of them—drug burnout, unwanted pregnancy, criminal record, etc. Did you ever just sit back and watch a baby learn about the stove or electrical outlets? Probably not! You probably ran to the rescue. But some children do learn the hard way and bear scars for life. Likewise, if you engage in some of the behaviors demanded by peer pressure, you could be scarred for life.

The adult world is very concerned about teenagers these days, and no wonder! Serious behavior and character problems seem to be destroying the adults of tomorrow. Why do teenagers succumb to the demands of the peer culture when they know the bad long-range consequences? This is where the generation gap is most painful. Adults cannot step into your skin. Only you as a teenager know what immense pressures are on you. But do you see where they are coming from and where they are taking you?

I cannot help but notice the mass commercialization of youthful ideals that has occurred since I was a teenager. Our society has become a "society on the take," and youth have been bribed into the role of consumers. They no longer have a voice in political affairs. When was the last time you saw an antiwar youth rally? Many teenagers feel powerless in this situation. If you have ideals beyond the immediate gratification of your own needs and wants, where can you take them? Teen power has been subtly replaced by teen culture, and peer pressure is its greatest sales agent. If you feel a lot of pressure to compromise your values, it is no wonder. That is the intention of an economy that needs you to consume.

Well, the last thing you need is more pessimistic appraisals of your situation. What most teenagers want is what most people want—a happy and meaningful life and a bright future. In Christ we know that is God's intention for us. That doesn't mean life won't be hard or painful. But it will have meaning and purpose and joy as well as pain, happiness as well as sadness, and serenity as well as anxiety. There is hope for the future and for your future.

*T*he Future and Friends

*T*he future lies in your becoming yourself. If you compromise your values, you will never become yourself, and you will have no future at all. The pressure to consume, conform, and compromise may overwhelm you.

God has endowed you with a conscience so you know right from wrong. You know whether you are doing the right thing or the wrong thing with your life. You may think of it merely as the best of choices or the worst of choices, but you know where you stand. Do you have the strength, however, always to make the right decision? Can you stand alone?

I sincerely believe that if Daniel had had one close friend—someone with whom he could have shared his true feelings—he would not have been overwhelmed by peer pressure. When we measure the value of human life, we can see how much Daniel lost. If a life were worth, for example, $1 billion for 75 years, then he blew about $80 million. If having one good friend could have prevented that, then we must admit that friendship is a very valuable thing, as valuable as life itself. A friend can make it so much easier to stand up for what you think is right. A friend can make it so much easier to be yourself.

One thing many teenagers don't realize is that Jesus is a Friend. Jesus is a Friend who will listen to your feelings and will support you in making difficult decisions. Jesus is not just a rubber stamp friend, however; He is a true Friend, because He will judge you if you do something against your values. Even if you don't accept Jesus as a Friend, you cannot escape His judgment, because He claims you as a friend whether you claim Him as one or not.

Jesus is not only a judging Friend. He is a forgiving Friend. He allowed Himself to be sacrificed for all of our wrong decisions, for all of our compromises, and for all of our sins. Because of that sacrifice, we are forgiven, and because He rose from the dead, Jesus Himself brings the gift of forgiveness. That means that no matter how much we have conformed to peer pressure or what bad things we have done to our lives in order to be popular or even acceptable, we always have our Friend (and Lord) who is ready to forgive us and help us start all over. In this continual friendship and forgiveness there is hope for the future. We do not have to be powerless slaves of the peer culture. We are freed up to be ourselves and step confidently into the future.

Jesus has a special place in His heart for those who are considered "nobodies." In the words of the popular T-shirt, Jesus knows we are somebody because "God don't make no junk." This slogan is particularly popular with minority persons because they are often considered "nobodies" in our society. In fact, the expression "I Am Somebody" was coined by the Rev. Jesse Jackson when he addressed black teenagers who felt they were being considered "nobodies." Jesus knows that the judgment of society and the loneliness and shame that go with it are enough for a "nobody" to bear. So He has deep compassion for the "nobodies" and offers His comfort and companionship to them.

I Building Friendships

I don't want to give you the impression that Jesus is the only friend you need. Jesus Himself surrounded Himself with friends, particularly in times of stress. On the night He was arrested, when the pressures on Jesus were almost enough to make Him explode, He called His friends around Him and went out into the garden to pray. Of course, you know the story. Jesus' friends couldn't stay awake. Don't forget, however, these were the men whom God later used to start the greatest "social institution" that has ever existed—the church. That is the type of miraculous future that faith unfolds.

So you need to build some solid friendships in your life. These friends won't be perfect, but then neither will you. Your life would be richer if you had friends of both sexes. A boyfriend or a girlfriend shouldn't prevent you from having other friends, even of the opposite sex. (A true test of loyalty in a serious relationship is if you can trust each other with friends of the opposite sex.)

How can you go about developing friendships? For some this is easier than for others. There is no way around that. When Daniel tried to win his way into the popular group, he was looking at friendship as a means to an end. He was mainly interested in what he could get out of his friendships. Daniel probably never thought of it the other way around. He probably never thought he had anything to give. His opinion of himself, which was based on what his peers thought of him, was pretty low. This is a common situation, and if you feel that way, you may have difficulty in making friends. The way to overcome this difficulty is to believe that you have something to give. If you really cannot find anything in yourself that you can give to another for the sake of friendship, perhaps you should take this concern to the one Friend you always have with you.

Everyone has something to give. We are created with the capacity to love, and though selfishness seems to make love impossible, Jesus has reopened that possibility to us. Love really is the answer, and because you can love, you can reach out with confidence to make a friend.

It is good advice not to look for friends among those who are compromising their values for the sake of popularity because, like Daniel, they are regarding friendship as a step to some goal. Once made, friendships require maintenance. It is necessary to reinforce your friends for some things and to criticize them for others. If you are not able to do both, your friendship will be lopsided and shallow.

Most important, though, it is necessary to forgive. Just as forgiveness is central to the relationship between God and ourselves, so is forgiveness central to all human relations. "Be kind to one another, tenderhearted, forgiving one another, as God in Christ forgave you" (Eph. 4:32). Your friends will let you down, and you will let your friends down. Such is human nature. Forgiveness allows friendships to continue despite failures.

Can you imagine what the world would be like if people were all friends to each other like this? Can you imagine a world where everyone loves everyone else—not with phony, selfish love, but with forgiving love—where friendships outlast our failures? This is exactly the kind of world God envisions for us. If this were not the case, then we would have to admit that Jesus lived and died in vain. Yet this kind of world is only a hope. It is not going to happen overnight. You know how much time, effort, and skill go into a good friendship. But if everyone knew the possibilities of friendship, if everyone reached out to make friends—. Think about it.

*T*HINGS YOU CAN DO

Individual: Sharpen your questioning and listening skills with an experiment in friend-making. In this exercise you can practice the skills of making and keeping friends without having an actual friendship at stake. Choose someone you know and try the following experiment. Ask them questions about themselves for five minutes, always either listening or asking a new question. The object of the experiment is to see if they notice your intentional behavior and if it has a positive effect on them. The challenge of the experiment is to see if you can pull it off without them noticing anything unusual. Another minor challenge is to see how few questions you can get by with in five minutes of questioning-listening. After you have mastered this with someone you know, try it, still as an experiment, with someone you do not know. Compare your results.

Group: Discuss in your group what makes a person popular in your school. Someone can write these characteristics on a blackboard or poster. Make another list of what makes a person unpopular. Roleplay an unpopular person. Do this in two stages: First, have two persons demonstrate in front of the whole group. One plays the part of the unpopular person, and the other plays the part of someone trying to make friends with an unpopular person. After you have done this once, divide into pairs and each take a turn at each part. After 10 minutes or so (five minutes for each part) return to the group and discuss the experience. You might bring up key questions like these: Do you think you have anything in common with an unpopular person? Is your group one in which newcomers would feel pressure to prove themselves? What kinds of things did you talk about to establish friendship with an unpopular person? Is your group a clique or is it open to anyone?

4

Parents and Family

*H*ave you been to a wedding and heard the pastor say, "For this reason a man shall leave his father and mother and be joined to his wife" (Mark 10:7)? Of course, the same would apply to a woman. *For this reason*—while it may seem that this reason is marriage, actually the overall reason is adulthood, since marriage is for adults. Leaving father and mother is a *separating*. First, you separate from your mother's womb at birth, and second, you separate from your father and mother for adulthood. The later separation doesn't happen all at once like at birth, but rather is a process spread out over several years. Those several years are known as adolescence or the teen years. During this time you are forming your own identity in distinction from your identification with your parents. Because of this it can be a time also of stormy parent-youth relationships.

Jan and Her Mother

*J*an's relationship with her mother was particularly stormy. In fact, her high school principal arranged a conference with both Jan and her mother because of Jan's poor attendance at school. As the principal tried to get mother and daughter working together, Jan said, "She doesn't care about me—why should I listen to her?"

Before her mother could defend herself, the principal said, "Jan, who took care of you when you were sick?"

Jan lowered her eyes. "She did," she said, motioning toward her mother.

"Who prepared your food as you were growing up?"

"I suppose Mom."

"You suppose?" asked the principal.

"Nah, she did."

"And where have your clothes come from—and how did they get clean?"

"Ok!" said Jan with some exasperation, "It was Mom!"

The principal paused and then said, "So your mom has spent a lot of time and energy caring for you during these years. That doesn't sound like she doesn't care."

What the principal was doing was raising some questions we can easily forget when we see only our parents' shortcomings. Of course, there is a lot more that needs attention in Jan's relationship with her mother, and her mother also needs help. Being a parent of teenagers is about as tough as being a teenager, but there are also rewards in both experiences. [I am writing to you as a parent who can still recall the teenage years from my own adolescent perspective. I am also writing from the perspective of a parent in terms of my own teenage children. I hope this double perspective will be helpful to you in getting insight into whatever needs you have in regard to your family.]

H Running Away

*H*ave you ever felt like running away? Jan tried it, but the police brought her back. Over 150,000 young people run away from home each year in this country, and some never return. Some run because of unendurable abuse in their homes. Others are like Jan—she and her mother had gotten into a quarreling relationship which neither could seem to change. Most of us in our teen years confine our running away to fantasy. We do trial runs in our mind. We fantasize about how this would cause a crisis with our parents, as it did for Jan's mother. We know our running away would shake our parents up—or at least we hope it would. It would get us the kind of care we feel we are missing. It is also a way of getting back at them.

When we can cause our parents to worry about us, we are exercising power over them. In this way we are affirming our own distinct identity. But why are parents so vulnerable? Why would they care? The only answer is because they do. But we are not always sure of this, and so we provoke a crisis for reassurance.

A more drastic form of running away is the suicide attempt. It is dangerous to attempt suicide because one may not be able to control the attempt and actually do it. Fantasizing suicide can be similar to fantasizing running away when one is trying to shock parents into caring. While these fantasies are understandable when one feels unloved and angry, there are better ways of coping with this problem.

*W*Taking the Baggage Along

*W*hen we run away from home, either in fantasy or reality, we are actually taking the "home baggage" with us, and it needs to be left behind. You will ultimately need to leave father and mother, but running away is not the same as leaving. In his radio show Garrison Keillor reminisced over his upbringing in the fantasy world of Lake Woebegone. At age 14 he was attracted to the ceremonious worship of the Roman Catholic Church, which was in direct contrast to the plainness of the services in his Plymouth Brethren Church. He told Father Emil that he wanted to leave his own church and become a Catholic. Father Emil was understanding with him but declined to accept his overture. "You will have to leave home sometime," he said, "but you have to know where home is before you can leave it. And at 14 you are not there yet." The better ways of coping with family stress are ways of getting to know where home is so you can really leave it.

Leaving is a process of becoming yourself, and when it is completed, you can leave without taking the home baggage with you. This home baggage is your dependency, and this dependency makes it impossible really to leave. Rebelling—even running away—does not remove this dependency, even though it looks like it would. It actually confirms it. The anger, resentment, and rejection that you feel at these times are all part of dependency. Instead of leaving father and mother, you take your resentment with you—and so you are still not free to leave.

*Y*Learning from Family Problems

*Y*ou can learn a lot about yourself from your family problems. Since what you learn is valuable data for your maturing process, such learning is a good substitute for running away. Such learning is also an alternative to other destructive ways of coping with these problems.

One of the more common destructive ways of coping is pitting your parents against each other. If your parents differ, for example, on how they should discipline you, or if one gives in easily and the other is strict, it is tempting to play one off against the other. These are destructive ways because they chip away at your parents' marital relationship.

Another destructive way of coping is to take out your resentment on your brothers and sisters. The younger ones particularly are easy scapegoats for such projecting. Yet younger siblings also know the subtle ways in which they can nettle their older siblings. These actions are destructive because they undermine the spirit of cooperation in the family and also further frustrate your parents.

One thing that may come through to you as you seek to learn from your problems with your parents is that a decided change may have taken place in your attitude toward your parents. When you were a child, you probably thought more highly of your parents than you do now. In fact, you may have placed them on an unrealistic pedestal. Your parents were your first image of God. This is why you asked them so many questions, and the only answer that ever troubled you was "I don't know." After all, being like gods they were supposed to know!

Now there has been a change. They have fallen from this pedestal, and their fallen image in your teenage mind can be just as unrealistically low as it previously was unrealistically high. This is what the school principal was attempting to show Jan. The maturing process in your teen years has as one of its goals that you see the true identity of your parents. This is basic to the shaping of your own identity.

I Beyond Two-Parent Families

have been referring to *parents*, assuming you have two of them. But some of you may have just one—or are at least living with only one. The number of one-parent households is increasing. By 1994 it is anticipated that 40 percent of teenagers will not be living with both of their natural parents. Jan lives only with her mother. She vaguely remembers her father before he left the family and her parents were divorced. She doesn't even know where he is. She feels cheated, and she takes out some of her resentment on her mother. Jan also feels rejected. Why did her father abandon her?

Others of you may have a parent who died, and you also may feel cheated. Your anger over this may be subconsciously directed toward God for taking your parent—why me? The parent who remains after the death or divorce of the other has similar feelings. Why has she/he been left alone to rear the children? It would be good for both parent and teenager if they could talk about their similar feelings, but they rarely do. Therefore they just as rarely understand the other's feelings. Parents may have their own problems, which have little to do with their relationship with their children, yet they carry their feelings about these problems into the family. The children misunderstand and believe they are the cause of the trouble.

Yet children in one-parent families have one advantage over those with two parents who are in doubt about their care. Jan at least knew where she stood—her father has abandoned her. When, however, one is in doubt about a parent's care, one may feel the need to test it—by running away, for example.

Some of you may have two parents, neither of whom are your biological parents. As an adopted child, you may, without knowing the circumstances, wonder why your biological parents left you. You might even wish you could meet them so that you could ask them. But your adopted parents are also your real parents. We are influenced in our development as much or more by our environment as by our heredity. Your biological parents have simply sired you; your adopted parents are rearing you. Realistically, you don't have to meet your "real" parents because you are living with them.

W **Your Heavenly Parent**

hether you are in a single-parent family through death or divorce or were born to an unwed mother, or whether you are living with two parents, adopted or not, and wondering if one or the other really loves you, or whether you are living with two parents and feel secure in their love—you are all the same in another way. You all have the same heavenly Parent and belong to the same heavenly family. You all have equal access to this heavenly Parent because He loves each as He loves the others.

It is no coincidence that God is called Father—a term of parenthood. He is our Creator who made us in His image. He is also love itself and therefore loves us as His children because it is His nature to love. Even the best of human parents—if such could be recognized—loves imperfectly because he or she is flawed by sin. God is also a Parent to your parent or parents. We do not grow out of *this* parental dependency, nor need we leave this Parent to mature. Rather we grow *in* this dependency because He is God, and we are His creation.

Parents pray to their heavenly Parent about the problems they are experiencing in their relationship with *their* children. Children do the same in regard to their relationship with their parents. I have found comfort in the realization that my children could and can go to their heavenly Parent with their concerns about me and my relationship with them. I am well aware of at least some of my parental shortcomings—as are most parents—though we rarely let our children know this. God's forgiveness is also for me—and for other parents and for you and for all other children. He is the only perfect One—the only secure One. For this reason we can be perfectly honest with Him since He has no fragile ego.

Because He is God, you and I can hope. Whatever stress you are experiencing now, including stress with your parents, will pass. When we feel hopeless, we tend to read "foreverness" into the present stress. If instead we follow the psalmist's advice and "wait for the Lord," our hope is restored. He can use your present stress as a way of teaching you to know more about yourself, about your parents, and about your relationship with them. You can learn from it and grow in maturity.

*D*o you know the Serenity Prayer used by *Alcoholics Anonymous*?
If you belong to Alateen, you know it well. But this prayer applies to far more than alcoholism. You can use it as a prayer in family stress. It goes like this:

> Lord, grant me the serenity to accept the things that cannot be changed, the courage to change the things that can, and the wisdom to know the difference.

The prayer is based on a recognition that this is a fallen world inhabited by fallen people. Not every desire we have for change is going to come about because we pray for it. Though "with God all things are possible," God also adjusts His powers to protect the freedom and responsibility of His people. The plain fact is that barring some drastic change in their lives, some parents seem either unwilling or unable to give their children the love that they really need. The tragedy is that there are people in midlife who are still trying to receive this love in one form or another from one or both of

41

their own parents and are frustrating their own maturing and development because they do not seem to be able to leave father and mother until they receive their love.

The good news for these people is that they do not have to receive their parents' love in order to leave them. They can receive this love instead from their heavenly Parent and from His family, the church. When they receive this love, they can accept the limitations of their parents—"accept the things that cannot be changed."

The separation of families into isolated units puts too much responsibility on parents to meet all the needs of their children for adult relationships. At the same time there are too many pressures on children, especially teenagers, to satisfy all of their parents' ambitions. Both parents and children need to belong to a larger family in which these responsibilities can be shared with others. Your church can be this larger family where you can relate to other adults than your parents, and your parents can relate to other children than their own.

The prayer for "serenity to accept the things that cannot be changed" applies not only to extremely deficient parental relationships but to all parental relations. All parents have difficulties in loving and caring. The difference is only in degree. When you accept the fact that your parents are sinful human beings like everyone else, you are accepting "the things that cannot be changed." Put in the positive, this means that you are accepting them the way they are—which is precisely the way that God accepts you. I hope it is also the way your parents accept you.

Forgiveness makes it possible for us to do this for each other. It all begins with God. As we are forgiven by Him, we can forgive others—even our parents and brothers and sisters—and they can forgive us. Just as important, we can forgive ourselves. "We love, because He first loved us" (1 John 4:19).

But there is also the petition for courage to change the things that can be changed. God may not have given us the power to change others, but He has given us the power to change ourselves. Your parents may need more help from you to improve your relationship. They probably also feel bad about the state of things. Speaking humorously as a frustrated parent of teenagers, someone has said, "In real life, we parents embarrass our teenagers by our existence."

If you want a different response from your parents, you may have to provide a different stimulus. What are you asking them to do to improve your relationship with them? What are some things that you could do that your parents would appreciate? You know them well enough to come up with some ideas. We will deal with these when we discuss "Things You Can Do" at the close of this chapter.

Now how can you know the difference between the things that can be changed and the things that cannot? This is why we pray for wisdom. God may need to use others to give you this wisdom. I would suggest you seek counsel on this question. Don't be surprised if the counselor you go to—whether at church or school—wants to talk with your parents as well. The school principal wanted to talk with Jan and her mother. There is good reason for this. Having your parents—or even your brothers and sisters—with you helps to keep all of you more honest. The counselor also needs to see things for himself or herself. Let's face it: Your description of what is going on at home is probably slanted; so is that of your parents. It is in seeing the real thing, namely, you and your parents together in action, that the counselor sees what none of you can see simply because you are all too close to the scene. This is why wisdom is often lacking in family affairs and why families may need outside help to get a clearer perspective of what is happening in their family relationships.

Significantly, it was the principal who initiated the conference with Jan and her mother, and he did so because of a crisis in Jan's school attendance. Why do we always wait for a crisis to do something about our problems and then let an adult take the initiative to do something about it? When you are feeling intense pressure over things, remember that you have the option yourself to initiate the helping process. Please consult the appendix for procedures in securing a skilled and competent counselor.

Difficulties in Initiating the Leaving Process

*H*ow does one initiate the "leaving process"? It is not easy for either you or your parents to do this. If you rebel against your parents, would this not be a way of taking leave of them? In some respects it is. It can also be a way of getting stuck. Some people never seem to get beyond rebelling. Even in midlife they are still resisting anybody in authority over them who reminds them of their parents. They are compulsive rebellers.

At the opposite extreme are those who conform to their parents' ideas. Just as rebels see only their parents' faults, conformists see only their virtues. You can get stuck also in conforming.

Even in midlife these conformists feel guilty if they have differing ideas from their parents'.

Conforming to your parents' ideas is not the same as obeying them. You may disagree with your parents over what time you should be in, but out of respect for their parental authority, you may still get in at that time. Conforming young people on the other hand won't admit to any disagreement. They are like young people who have joined religious cults and feel they must defend the parent figure cult leader at all costs.

This will be a problem if they should later marry, because their mates will see only too clearly the faults of their inlaws. When they say so, what happens? The conforming children defend their parents, because if they acknowledge their faults, they would in their own minds be disobedient, disloyal, and ungrateful. If they haven't left their original home, how then can they form a new one?

I don't believe that conforming young people are really unaware of their parents' shortcomings. Rather I believe they are afraid that if they admitted this to themselves, they would have to face their hidden resentment of their parents. At the moment this is too threatening to deal with.

The commandment that God has given us to honor our father and mother does not mean that we must think they are perfect. You don't think the same now as you did when you were a child. Then you could not see your parents' shortcomings. Now you see them, perhaps exaggeratedly so. As a teenager, however, you still continue to honor your parents by accepting them as they are. By doing so you recognize that you still need them—to guide you, to dialog with you, and even to argue with you. This kind of honoring makes it normal ultimately to leave your parents. If you can't honor them in this way, how will you be able to honor the authorities in the structures of our society—bosses, government leaders, church authorities—under whom you will live your entire life?

Your parents on the other hand may find it hard to let you go because they hold on to the memory of how you were as a child. Like most parents they probably don't appreciate the changes that adolescence brings. They may have difficulty seeing the difference between your obedient behavior and your disagreement with their ideas. You may have some arguments, but this won't hurt you or them.

We parents have a mental picture of what our children should be like, and we need to let go of this picture so that our children can

44

be free to leave. Just as it is hard for you as a teenager to accept your parents as they are, warts and all, so it is also hard for your parents to accept you as you are, particularly when you differ from what they had pictured you would be.

Friends of the Future

*Y*our parents are your friends of the future. Really! In one sense this is what it means to leave them. You leave them as parental authorities and join them again as peers—friends. It helps if you keep this in mind when things look bleak in your parental conflicts. At these times remember that you are not the same person you were— nor should you be—and also that the transition between who you were and who you are becoming is hard for your parents. It really indicates the transition from their mental image of what you should be like to the real you.

They will make it! So hang in there because you will make it, too. You will grow to see your parents as they really are and will accept them. Why am I so confident about this? Because God wants it this way. It is part of His creative plan for you and your family, and He will help you both. Of course, you and your parents can frustrate His help, and it won't be easy. However, there is a marvelous reward ahead for all of you, children and parents, as you become friends with each other. It is worth all the trouble you may both be going through in reaching it. If your relationship with your siblings is also stormy, you might keep in mind that they too will likely become your friends in adulthood.

The Family of God

*A*lthough you are headed for the time when you will be leaving your parental home, such is not the case regarding your larger family. As my children were growing into adulthood, I was pleased when they developed relationships with other adults, particularly those who were good models. We all need a larger family, and, as stated previously, your church can serve in this capacity. Being *the* responsible adults in your life places too much of a demand on your parents. Help them out by getting involved with others who can share this responsibility: your pastor, Sunday school teacher, scout leader, church youth leader, or even the parents of your friends. For a hopeful future in the family of God you need friendships not only with your peers but also with persons of other generations—despite the social pressures against this. Your parents also may take an interest in other kids, such as your friends. They too need this extra adult attention though it may seem they are sharing what belongs to you.

When you leave father and mother, you will stay in your larger family but with a new status, namely as an adult who cares about the children in this family as a support to their own parents. This is one of the ways that you as a member of a Christian congregation—or, as St. Paul put it, a member of the body of Christ—can give support to the other members.

*T*HINGS YOU CAN DO

Individual: By now you have probably thought of some things you can do that would please your parents. At least you can think of some things you can *stop* doing that irritate them. If the things you think of involve nothing against your moral or spiritual convictions, focus on doing them for a 24-hour period. In other words, block out a day in which you put your best efforts into the relationship.

Doing these things for just 24 hours is within your possibility, but it may not be long enough to get a response. Yet it is good practice in directing yourself—in exercising the freedom that God has given you.

Next try the same thing for a 48-hour period. This may be enough to receive at least *some* encouragement. A young woman shared with me the time that she put her arms around her mother and told her she loved her: "Mother and I had not been getting along, and there was very little affection between us. I decided I would take the initiative and give her a hug. She was so startled she stiffened up. A couple of days later I did it again. This time I could feel her body loosen. The third time she hugged me back."

For your third effort try a 72-hour period and see what *you* notice.

Group: Your church youth group could sponsor a teen-parents dialog once or twice a year. I have been involved in several of these and have witnessed some excellent results. After the youth and their parents come together at the church, they divide into their own groups with an appointed leader. Each group shares its concerns in the parent-teen relationship and formulates suggestions to be presented to the combined group. After a break the parents and youth meet together to dialog on the suggestions of each. The purpose is to decide jointly on actions that the families can take to improve relationships.

At its regular meeting your youth group can be a support with family problems. As people share their concerns, they soon discover they are not the only ones having such difficulties. With good leadership the sharing can move into constructive suggestions. Roleplaying a parental conflict can provide helpful insights also. If you take your parents' role, you will begin to feel as they do, and this empathy will help you in the actual relationship. Another thing you can do is practice being counselors to each other. Ask one of the group to be your counselor as you share the problem. Please refer to the appendix concerning the format for peer counseling.

5

Growth in Sexuality

*H*elen was flattered when Bob began to date her. He was 25—so much more mature than boys her own age. She felt she was more mature, too, just from dating Bob. Helen had had crushes on other boys but nothing like this. She had not previously engaged in sexual intercourse and did not plan to do so with Bob. Bob was not really as mature as Helen thought, but he was *experienced*. When he made his move for intercourse, Helen let her common sense go. Later she realized she was probably fertile when it happened.

Helen's is an old and familiar story, but when it happens, it is all brand new. When she realized she was pregnant, she told Bob, hoping against hope that he would have an answer. He was sympathetic but definitely not interested in getting married. He did say, however, that she could move in with him. This was not what Helen had hoped for.

Fortunately for Helen, she had parents she felt she could go to in her distress. They were naturally upset and disappointed when she told them, but after the initial shock, her mother suggested that they call the pastor. He came that evening and helped them make some initial decisions about how they would cope with the situation.

Sex Is a Natural Function

*H*elen's story may give the impression that sex is bad. Sexual desire is a strong emotion, and it frightens some people, but sexual activity is a natural human function. God created us as sexual beings, male and female. In this respect He fashioned us like the rest of His creatures. Our sexual endowment is the basis for mating and reproduction. "God saw everything that He had made, and behold, it was very good" (Gen. 1:31).

Sex is not sinful. It is necessary to say this in a religious book because too often people have received the opposite impression from their religious teaching. How we *use* sex may be sinful, but that is another matter. As we love our bodies, so we can also love our sexual nature.

Although God created us as sexual beings like other forms of life, there is a distinct difference between our sexuality and that of these other forms. Animals are governed in sexuality by instinct; reproduction is the goal of mating. Humans are able to make decisions; more than reproduction is involved in sexuality. Some people, however, also consider human sex to be instinctually governed, and this attitude leads to the *dehumanizing* of sexual activity.

The idea that we are like the animals in our sexuality was previously associated with the double standard on sexual morality. Men supposedly had more sexual desire than women, and so they acted more on instinct like animals. Women, on the other hand, had less sexual desire; they were able to make decisions regarding their sexual behavior.

These ideas about men and women are changing rapidly, and for this we can be grateful. Women are now recognized as sexual beings with similar sexual desires as men. We are finally understanding more clearly who we were created to be.

The "sexual revolution" has also ended the double standard about who is governed by instinct. While this may be good, many in our culture have unfortunately moved in the direction of emphasizing instinct on the part of both men and women. They missed the opportunity to go the other way, namely, to see that men and women are both capable of making decisions regarding their sexual desires. Whether you are male or female, you do not have to act by instinct. If you decide not to follow through on your desires, that does not mean you are sexually or personally deficient—in spite of media attempts to suggest this.

A genuine sexual revolution would liberate both men and women to be fully human. God can lead us further than our culture. We can affirm our sexuality as good and direct it according to our values.

Animals have an instinct that directs their sexual functions in the direction God intended. We humans lack these instinctual protections. We don't know by instinct the right time and the right conditions. Human sexual desire needs to be directed just like all other desires, in order to keep it healthy and good. Like all other desires, it can be used either constructively or destructively. In order to direct our sexual desires, we have to make decisions. It is our values that help us to make these decisions wisely. Our values are part of our identity; they make up who we are. By the same token, our identity is shown through our values.

Cultural Pressures for Premarital Sex

While we are not governed by instinct, we are unfortunately subject to cultural pressures. As we have discussed in a previous chapter, these cultural pressures for teenagers are experienced as peer pressure. In this instance it is the pressure to experience sexual intercourse. Letting these pressures direct us is a poor substitute for decision making.

Our culture likes to claim it is enlightened about sex, but actually it is not. We know lots of facts, but we don't know how to relate them to values. Some sex education is a case in point. In dealing with birth control, for example, the decision about when and where to use the facts is left with the individual. When the use of birth control measures is described in a supposedly value-neutral way, many perceive an implicit permission or even encouragement to engage in premarital intercourse.

I agree that it is better to know the facts than to be caught unexpectedly in a situation like Helen's. Helen did know the facts, but at that moment her knowledge didn't seem to matter. The availability of the birth control pill and other contraceptive means has not reduced teenage pregnancies. Something other than knowledge is needed. I suggest it is a sense of values. Your values are the personal priorities by which you make your decisions.

Our culture's interpretation of sexuality equates it with sexual intercourse. It is also implied that one hasn't really lived until one has had this experience. Both of these ideas are illusions, yet you and your peers may assume that they are true. Would not many movies lead you to believe this?

The media use these ideas to put on the pressure. Your way of qualifying with your peers—of being "in"—is to have sex. They probably even bluff a good bit about their experiences, because they would not want anyone to know how inexperienced they really are.

50

To be a male or female virgin is to be "out of it." This kind of pressure doesn't allow much freedom to make your own decisions, does it?

Not everybody enjoys their first sexual experience. First times for anything are usually not that good. But some do enjoy it. If sex is enjoyable, and if God made it to be enjoyable, why would anyone want to put controls on it? Are those who talk about controls only trying to deprive you of pleasure? Is it possible? Some people, even religious people, are suspicious, even frightened, of pleasure. But don't look on everyone who mentions controls as having that attitude. Some of us want you to have pleasure that is in accordance with God's design and will, and that is more than just for the moment.

Love and Lust

*O*ur sexual feelings can be characterized by very different attitudes. One is the attitude of love in which we reach out to a person of the opposite sex with a desire to become one with the other—"one flesh" as the Scripture describes it. We desire to express this love totally—to share ourselves by sharing our body with the other. Love respects the other's space and personal identity.

The other attitude is lust. This is the desire to possess the other for oneself—to use the other for one's own selfish satisfaction. The common word used to express this attitude is *scoring* and that is itself a giveaway. It is like scoring points in a game. One has made a conquest, has exercised control over another. Sexual lust is really the lust for power over others.

Jesus' familiar reference to adultery as an act of the heart as well as of the body pertains to this attitude. "I say to you that everyone who looks at a woman lustfully has already committed adultery with her in his heart" (Matt. 5:28). The same would be true, of course, for a woman. To look lustfully at another does not refer primarily to our daydreams or to our sleep dreams but to an attitude coming from our heart that views others as objects to possess or to use.

Sexuality and Self-Development

*T*here is much more to sexuality than sexual intercourse. Our sexuality is inseparable from our person. It shows itself in our desire for closeness with others. The warmth that you feel toward others—

51

for example, your caring about them and your affection toward them—is all a part of your sexuality. The hug, the kiss, the arm around the shoulder, and the touch are ways by which we include our bodies in our caring.

Our sexuality is also expressed in our deep religious feelings. Many of our popular songs express a love and affection that is spiritual in nature. When we grow in our faith, we direct these songs to Jesus since we realize that He is the source of this love. Our hymns express our love and affection toward Jesus as well as His toward us. This is understandable since He is described in the Bible as our Friend and the Bridegroom of the church.

Sexuality may be expressed through sexual intercourse, but it is also expressed in broader dimensions as we enjoy the warmth, affection, and closeness of our cherished personal relationships. In fact, from a Christian point of view sexual intercourse is a celebration of a loving and affectionate relationship between a male and a female who have committed themselves to each other for life. This commitment is made in marriage. When we are close to another and in that relationship desire sexual intercourse, this act provides us with inexpressable satisfaction.

For your sexuality to be an integral part of your development as a person, you need to devalue and resist cultural pressures and be what God intends you to be. Having sexual relations with another and being close to him or her as a person are not necessarily the same. Sexual activities can actually be used as a substitute for closeness, settling for physical pleasure rather than personal intimacy. For personal closeness our sexual nature needs to be governed by values that cultivate such closeness. Since there really is nothing to prove in being sexually experienced, once you see through the folly of cultural pressure, you can be free to wait for it.

Your sexual development is nothing to fear. It is programmed into you by your Creator, and as He said, it is very good. Learning to wait is known as discipline. Despite the bad vibes this word may have for you, discipline is really your friend. It is the way you exercise your freedom to follow God's design for you.

Negative Experiences

Sex may seem like anything but good to those who are hurt by it. Helen, for example, went through a lot of heartache because of one sexual experience. Yet Helen is fortunate. Because of the support she received, she again feels positive about sex. She knows she can profit from her experience and direct herself more wisely in the future.

Others who are hurt, however, get bogged down in guilt and repeat their mistakes. If they are girls, they become known as "available"; if they are boys, they become known as "wanting just one thing." Few recognize that below the surface these labeled persons feel a defilement that prevents them from making a change.

Some hurts are inflicted early by incest. Children are sexually abused by their own parents or other family members. Maybe it happened to you. Others know the terror of being forced—of rape. One feels violated when this happens, and this is an accurate assessment. One may also feel irreparably damaged. As one girl put it, "I must be a whore." The problem with the labels we give ourselves is that they can become self-fulfilling prophecies. The damage done by these negative experiences of sex is to our self-esteem—and self-esteem is reparable!

Sexual attacks can also happen to boys, particularly those of a homosexual nature. As with girls who have negative experiences, boys are also reluctant to tell anyone about them. They feel that they have been defiled by the act. This is especially true if they experience any pleasure in it. The feeling may be, "I must be gay because I enjoyed or even consented to this sex act."*

---

* There is a lot of understandable confusion about homosexuality. In spite of all the attention it has received, we are not sure what causes it or even what it is. It is likely that there is a combination of causes rather than one single cause. Some refer to it as an alternative life-style. The Bible regards homosexual behavior or activity as sinful. We have a choice regarding our actions. But do we have a choice regarding our preferences?

What really is a sexual preference? A preference, for example, can be more than how we feel. Even what we enjoy does not determine our identity any more than it determines right and wrong. Homosexual fantasies, dreams, desires, and even experiences, do not make one homosexual. In fact, these experiences have happened to many people who rightly consider themselves heterosexual. A recent study revealed that those who are considered heterosexual may have homosexual as well as heterosexual fantasies, and those who are considered homosexual may have heterosexual as well as homosexual fantasies.

From my own experience I am inclined to follow the research of Masters and Johnson. This research indicates that, these homosexual desires that cause us discomfort are related to particular influences that are present or lacking in our lives. The same is probably true of heterosexuality. By changing the influences one can change the direction of one's sexuality, but only when one is highly motivated to do so.

If any of these negative sexual experiences have happened to you or to a friend of yours, let me assure you that such an experience will not irreparably harm you. I know from talking with people who have been the victims of sexual abuse that they feel terribly hurt and utterly alone. The person responsible for these experiences is often an adult in a respected position of authority. God never intended for people to do things like incest and rape to other people. As hard to believe as it may be at the time, God grieves with you. He cares deeply about what has happened and will heal your spirit.

Your primary objective is your development as a person. Self-hatred because of negative sexual experiences can be your big enemy. In fact, these experiences increase any negative feelings about yourself that were already present. What you need are good feelings about yourself. Your challenge is to develop your confidence—your self-esteem. Work at your social skills that we discussed in a previous chapter so that you feel at ease with people of your own and of the opposite sex. The main thing to remember is that you are not doomed to anything because of your experiences. You have options. Believing this will influence the decisions you make.

What picture of yourself do you have in mind toward which you want to grow? Who are you motivated to be and to become? The most important factor in determining who you are is motivation. Guilt over any of your negative experiences or even fantasies can cause you to repeat them. This is why forgiveness is so important to your development.

We must deal constructively with our guilt. Otherwise it will become the destructive influence that shapes us the most. You may need to consult with someone you trust and whose values you respect in order to break your bondage to guilt. Forgiveness is the way we all maintain our identity as God's children, for we all need it continuously. Starting over is always possible through Christ. In fact, He is calling us to be renewed. We don't have to "twist His arm" or beg for His help. He wants us to be free from negative feelings about ourselves.

Forgiveness is more than just a gift we receive from God, for the Giver Himself comes with this gift. God is not only the one who forgives; He is also our Helper. In Christ He is our heavenly Friend with whom we can talk, even in our darkest moments, for He said, "Lo, I am with you always, to the close of the age" (Matt. 28:20).

A Time to Plan

s stated previously, sexuality is also connected with reproduction. Not everyone has children or even marries, but it is through mating and reproducing that the human family carries on. Although your developing years before marriage are the time to wait for sexual intercourse, they are a time to plan for the future.

Now is the time to begin planning your family. What kind of a person would you want to marry and have children with? What kind of a person should you be? Develop a model as your goal to grow into.

You are not the only one concerned here. Your actions affect others—even the unborn. This is because God has made us to be interdependent. Being aware of this helps us to be responsible persons. The kind of a *parent* you hope to be *then* has something to do with the kind of a *person* you want to be *now*.

Respect for what God has made means that we respect our bodies, as we saw in a previous chapter. It also means respecting those who may come out of our bodies. The decisions that we make about our sexuality are a part of this respect. It is not only what we *do* with our bodies, however, that may affect the well-being of the next generation, but also what we *put into* them. This points us to the next chapter on the use of drugs.

T HINGS YOU CAN DO

Individual: Write all the qualities you desire in a wife or husband. Compare these qualities with those you possess. What qualities do you lack? Make these your requests in prayer. God is even more interested in your personal growth than you are. He desires to give. The problem may lie in your openness to receive what you pray for. You can begin by believing you have received it and seeing yourself as having it.

Group: Plan an auction. The items to be auctioned are various kinds of relationships. Pick an auctioneer who will ask for bids on the relationships described below. Each person has $5,000 to spend but can spend no more than $2,500 on any one relationship. Bids must open at no less than $50 and no more than $500. Each person receives the list of available relationships prior to the auction. After reflecting on the list, each prepares a possible budget of the $5,000. The following table lists the relationships to be auctioned and also serves as an individual's account sheet.

Auction Items	Initial Amount $5,000.00	Personal Bid Budget/Actual	Top Group Bid
A person who has a lot of money			
A person who has a perfect figure			
A person who is handsome or pretty			
A satisfying sexual relationship			
A happy marriage			
A new and exciting relationship whenever the feeling arises			
A person who is honest and trustworthy			
A person who is going to college			
A person who has a good sense of humor			
A person who has the same religious beliefs			
A person who has a good job			
A single life with many relationships			
A family and a good mate			
A person with the same recreational interests			
A loving warm person			
A kind and generous person			

The bidding process forces one to protect the items most valuable and to let go of the least valuable.

6

Drugs and Health

It Ain't My Style

I'll never forget her smiling face. It was no different from her usual smile—a natural, good-humored smile that said, "Life has its ups, and it has its downs, but in this one moment I, Mary Andrews, am enjoying myself." But it was a smile in a special situation. It was a smile that bridged the generation gap when Mary Andrews said, "It ain't my style." What a special and vibrantly alive person she is!

The generation gap sometimes seems bottomless and wide—too wide to ever bridge from either side and too deep to chance a crossing. But some people manage to cross it. Mary Andrews is one. At home with either her peers or adults, Mary highly values personal honesty and treating people with respect. Those are values that make her appreciated and respected on both sides of the generation gap.

It hasn't been easy for Mary, and this was one of those trying moments. She had to endure a lot of loneliness and boredom to maintain her values. She had so many friends that it seemed as if she could never be lonely or bored. But her friends always treated her as if she were more mature. They highly respected her and her company, but when it came to doing things that Mary felt uncomfortable with, such as parties where drugs were used, they didn't invite her. They often shared important things about their feelings with Mary but kept other things secret from her because they knew she would not approve. So Mary had a lot of friends who only shared part of themselves with her, and she spent a lot of time home alone on Friday and Saturday nights.

That is how I got to know Mary. From the start she took great interest in the church youth group I worked with. It was an alternative to sitting at home and being bored and lonely. The church also apparently valued many of the things that Mary valued, such as respect for others and personal honesty.

One night we were discussing drugs in the group. We always tried to keep the group open (Mary was a big help in this), so we had the entire spectrum of drug use represented in the room, from "burnouts" to "users" to "straights" like Mary. The arguments were flying fast and furious with both sides giving their opinions—long-range burn out vs. short-range highs, the danger of cancer vs. the danger of being bored to death, documented birth defects vs. government propaganda, alternatives to drug use vs. getting high and then doing the alternatives, etc. Finally, Mary jumped up and shouted, "Hold it! Hold it! I know what it is. I know why I don't use drugs. It ain't my style!" And then she smiled. The room was actually quiet for a while as that one sank in, and I really loved that teenager at that moment.

I'll never forget that smiling face because, for one brief instant, she found what is important to both sides of the generation gap, to both teenagers and adults. She found what is important to drug users and nonusers. In the face of all the obstacles and forces that would put her down, she affirmed the unique value of her own life, and she affirmed it as the reason to pursue her own individual life-style. She was a rebel among her peers. And then she smiled!

*T*here are many reasons for drug use. Reasons for Drug Use

*T*here are many reasons for drug use. They are quite different for adults and for teens. Most adults use drugs because of dependency or addiction. They choose not to go without the mood swing that their drug of choice gives them.

Teenagers, on the other hand, are usually new at drug use and have not had time to develop serious dependencies or addictions— though some have, as you are well aware. Teenagers may get involved with drugs to find excitement (fun), to experiment, to gain peer acceptance, to rebel against authority, or to escape from reality.

Using drugs for excitement is nothing new. The number of drugs available and the variety of experiences they provide *are* new. You are being exposed to the widest variety of mood-altering chemicals ever available for human consumption. Many drugs have long histories of use. Did you know that prehistoric human beings probably invented alcohol before they invented soap? Did you know that the word *assassin* is derived from the word *hashish* and refers to a group of terrorists in the Turkish Empire who used hashish to mentally prepare themselves for political assassinations? The fall of the Turkish Empire has been attributed to widespread marijuana use among its elite military corps, the Janizaries. The use of opium in China dates back to prehistoric times. Did you know that the fictional detective Sherlock Holmes was a cocaine user? Lewis Carrol, who wrote *Alice in Wonderland*, was influenced by mescaline. American Indians have a long history of psylocybin and mescaline use in religious ceremonies. But during no other time in history has there been such a variety of drugs, nor have they been so readily avilable to teenagers.

As you well know, the resurgence of drug use began with the introduction of synthetic hallucinogenic drugs such as LSD and the emergence of the hippy movement in the 1960s. At first the movement was strongly centered on the hallucinogenic drugs such as marijuana and LSD, and the use of other drugs such as alcohol and heroin was considered a symptom of social degeneracy. But by the 1970s there was a marked increase in the use of all drugs, and the distinction between the so called "mind-expanding" drugs and other drugs was blurred. *All* drugs were used among the young, less for mind expansion than for getting high and partying. In the late '60s LSD was not a party drug. Now it is almost exclusively a party drug. Excitement rates high among the motives for drug use among the young.

But experimentation is still a strong motivation for drug use, especially among teenagers. In the book *The Natural Mind* by Andrew Weil the author points out that there seems to be a natural desire in human beings, particularly children, to experiment with altering consciousness.* He cites the activities of spinning and of smelling gasoline and other solvents. Because drugs readily give a high, they serve this purpose. You might not think that drugs are available to children, but even if they cannot obtain harder drugs, they can get "high" from sweets and from caffeine. Although you may be angry that you cannot buy airplane glue without a note from your parents, that law is designed to protect children.

Dr. Weil added one very important footnote: "When you get the

* Andrew Weil, *The Natural Mind* (Boston: Houghton Mifflin, 1972).

message, hang up the phone!" When people don't hang up the phone—that is, when they continue to use drugs after they experience the novelty and the excitement—they are in danger of becoming dependent, or addicted. After dependency sets in, the thrill is usually gone, and the person uses drugs only to satisfy the dependency. Often that dependency also serves the purpose of allowing the user to escape reality.

Dr. Weil was not advocating the use of drugs. He was advocating not using drugs. For those who want to avoid drugs he advocated alternatives, particularly religion. We might also include academics and athletics as alternatives in which young people are interested.

Dr. Weil advocated religion because he felt religion meets the same needs that drug use does—needs for expanded consciousness and ultimate meaning in life. Unfortunately, he wrote before the destructive power of cults had become known in our society. He wrote before Jonestown. Many young people join cults for the same reasons they use drugs—to expand their consciousness or to find ultimate meaning in life. Because their search is so earnest and naive, it is easy for power-hungry persons to exploit them.

It is somewhat repetitive to list peer acceptance and rebellion against authority as reasons for using drugs. They are usually not the primary reasons, but they do contribute to drug use. For instance, if you decide not to use drugs or alcohol at a party, that decision can be made a lot harder by the attempts of your friends to persuade you to use. Have you ever wondered why they are so intent on getting you to join in their use? While misery loves company, perhaps guilt feelings demand it. As another example, you might be tempted to use drugs to alleviate boredom or loneliness—to do something exciting. It is also exciting to rebel—to risk being different. So your decision to use drugs for excitement could be amplified by the excitement of rebelling.

*T*he Rough Road

*T*he major pressure on you to use drugs, therefore, is to find excitement and to explore new ways to find value and meaning in life. Life is often depressing and unexciting, boring and lonely. It can seem to be going nowhere, to have no purpose other than for you to fulfill someone else's expectations. Your school years are years in which you acquire the necessary skills and knowledge to fill some useful position in society. Sometimes it doesn't seem like you are going to be a person of your own making. If you are in control at all, you seem to be making yourself into a "nowhere man" rather than a unique "somebody." No wonder you want to break out of the mold and try something new! Conforming to the monotonous and boring "just ain't your style!"

In the 1970s when drug use was escalating to enormous proportions, the prevention word was "alternatives." The suggestion was made to try something other than drugs to break out of the mold. Try something else to prove to yourself you are unique and alive. Try an exciting alternative as your style. While many teenagers readily picked up this suggestion and began developing their own particular alternatives such as athletics, academic achievement, and work, drug use continued to escalate. Why? One reason was that you have to take somebody else's word for the assumption that alternatives are better than drug use. A lot of teenagers, perhaps yourself included, don't want to take someone else's word for what is meaningful and valuable in life. Those determinations are too important for someone else to decide for you. You might feel you have to find out for yourself whether the alternatives can provide what seems to be missing in life or whether drugs can do it. Therefore, to be really, uniquely yourself—to do things in your own style—you might feel it is necessary to experiment with drugs.

While the affirmation of your own style—your unique self—is healthy, it is sometimes reckless. Consider this: How can you experience drug use at a level that will provide something of ultimate meaning, something that will help you to become your true self? You cannot just get your toes wet. You will have to dive in over your head—with the possibility of drowning! Knowing the stakes are this high, you might want to reconsider the alternatives.

There is something even deeper going on in drug use— something that reaches into the most inner sanctums of your self. It is the question of suffering. Like the opposite sex, suffering is something you can't live with, and you can't live without. Of course, no one wants to suffer, but sometimes the easy road just has no promise. It is the hard road that leads to your true and genuine self. The word used for "true and genuine" is authentic. It is the hard road that leads to authenticity. Though no one has yet proved it, we seem to have an internal mechanism that searches out and follows the harder road. Drugs give the illusion of being a hard road. They offer

61

a lot of heavy hazards—dependency, burnout, addiction, self-destruction.

The reason I was so thrilled at Mary Andrews' statement was not that Mary was saying "It's not my style to avoid the hard road." She was saying "It's not my style to go the unreal road." Mary chose the hard road. It is hard to endure boredom, loneliness, and negative peer pressure. She did not choose to grab for the thrills of the moment, nor did she choose to avoid the hard road of suffering. She chose to take the road that had the greatest possibility, hard as it was.

The latest surveys (1982) show that Mary Andrews' style may become the prevalent style among teenagers. For the first time since the late 1960s, drug use among teenagers declined. One of the early factors cited for this decline is hard economic times. Considering what has been said about following the hard road toward being somebody, what do you think about this reason?

E Factors in Drug Use

ven if the economic situation reaches the proportion of a depression, drug use will not disappear. You will still have to make the hard and lonely choice of whether or not you will use drugs. In order to make that decision, there are some important factors you should consider. These are biased factors because it is impossible to be entirely objective. Those who favor using drugs are not objective either, so it is good to hear both sides of the argument before making your decision.

The first of these factors is the classification of drugs. Mood-altering drugs are classified according to their effect on the central nervous system. The classes are stimulants, depressants, tranquilizers, narcotics, hallucinogens, and others. Examples of stimulants are nicotine, caffeine, and amphetamines (speed). Tranquilizers include valium, thorazine, phencyclidine (PCP or angel dust), and Quaaludes. Some narcotics are opium, morphine, heroin, and codeine. Among the hallucinogens are mescaline, psilocybin, LSD, DMT, and STP. Others include such diverse groups as antidepressants, solvents (like airplane glue and oven cleaner), amylnitrate, etc. Some drugs are hard to classify. These include two of the most commonly used, marijuana and cocaine, which seem to fit somewhere among hallucinogens, stimulants, and tranquilizers.

Drugs are either naturally occurring chemicals or synthetic. Naturally occurring drugs include nicotine, caffeine, alcohol, opium, morphine, codeine, mescaline, psilocybin, and marijuana (includes hash and THC). Some synthetic drugs are amphetamines (speed), barbiturates (downers), valium, thorazine, phencyclidine (PCP or angel dust), Quaaludes, heroin, LSD, DMT, and STP.

Drugs are either legal or illegal. Most of the illegal drugs (controlled substances) can be prescribed by doctors, however. Examples of legal drugs are alcohol, weak amphetamines, weak barbiturates, caffeine, nicotine, and weak narcotics. Some of the controlled substances are amphetamines, barbiturates, tranquilizers, most narcotics, and all hallucinogens. Certain hallucinogens are legal under certain conditions. American Indians can use marijuana, mescaline, or psilocybin in their religious ceremonies. In some states it is legal to possess small amounts of marijuana, but it is not legal to sell it.

Alcohol presents an interesting problem, one that teenagers should be aware of. It is one of the most dangerous and destructive drugs available. It is one of the few drugs that can kill brain cells. It is responsible for thousands of accidental and intentional deaths. If it were properly listed as a cause of death among young people, it would be number one. It also has a strong tendency toward dependency and even addiction, as the number of chronic alcoholics in our society demonstrates. Yet it is a legal drug. The question is not at what age our society should allow the purchase of alcohol. It is whether it should be sold at all, considering the havoc it wreaks on human health.

In 1919 the sale of alcohol was prohibited in the United States by the Eighteenth Amendment. But in 1933 prohibition was repealed because alcohol was still being sold and outlaws were making all of the money. Who is making and selling illegal drugs in the United States today? Who is making the money from illegal drugs? Would legalizing certain drugs be helpful as in the case of alcohol, or would it just contribute to more abuse? These are difficult decisions facing the American public. They are best made by people who are *not* under the influence of the drug in question.

There are different ways to take drugs. They are ingested, inhaled, injected, and taken as suppositories. Ingestion (taking by mouth) and inhalation (either through nose or mouth) are the most popular ways of taking drugs. These methods of administration do not in themselves pose any *immediate* danger to the user. Inhalation of smoke, however, has been shown to cause cancer. Often drugs are injected either intravenously or intramuscularly, for the purpose of increasing their effectiveness and the quickness of their effect, but many people have an aversion to the use of needles. One good reason to avoid needles is that they can transmit disease unless properly sterilized. One of the major causes of death for narcotics addicts is serum hepatitis, a deadly disease transmitted from person to person through the use of unsterilized needles.

There are two dosages to consider when using drugs—the effective dose and the toxic dose. The effective dose is the minimum amount needed to give the desired result (depending on the method of administration). The toxic dose is the dose that will either make you sick or kill you. Sometimes the margin of safety between the two doses is small. Alcohol, for example, has a small margin of safety. The toxic dose is only 4 to 6 times the effective dose, depending on how the effective dose is defined. Fortunately most people pass out before they can drink enough alcohol to kill themselves.

Drugs that have a wide margin of safety are the hallucinogens. The toxic dose is so high that they are virtually nontoxic drugs. This fact was used as propaganda by the early advocates of psychedelic drug use, such as Timothy Leary and Allen Ginsberg.

Setting the dosage of drugs is tricky and should be left to physicians and pharmacists. They would not handle street drugs at all because they could not be sure of the potency of their supply. Indeed, unless they did an analysis, they couldn't even be sure the drug contained what the supplier said it did.

Side Effects

*R*elated to toxicity is the phenomenon of side effects. Most drugs have more than one effect on the human body. Often the side effects are dangerous and undesirable. They can be either immediate and dramatic, such as nausea and hair falling out, or they may be long-range and subtle, such as memory loss and genetic damage. Dependency is certainly an undesirable side effect. One commonly used street drug is the animal tranquilizer PCP, or angel dust. It's side effects are well known and documented. It is known to disintegrate vital brain function and to produce long-term, even chronic, mental aberrations and defects. Its use should definitely be avoided because its side effects outweigh its beneficial effects, no matter how you measure them. I wouldn't even feed it to my cat!

Another factor to consider with street drugs is quality control. Most legally prescribed drugs are manufactured and distributed under extremely careful regulation and procedures. Street drugs are, for the most part, manufactured in substandard locations with inadequate equipment and by unqualified persons. The chance for error is great. In addition, the spraying of herbicides on fields by some governments has introduced toxic substances. Such is the case with the use of paraquat on marijuana, for example.

If you are a consumer of street drugs, you have no assurance of what they really contain. In a recent study at the University of Minnesota researchers found that most street drugs contain harmless substitutes, such as Vitamin C and sugar. Sometimes the substitutes are cheaper drugs. You could be using valium, thinking it was cocaine—a deadly mistake if mixed with alcohol—or worse, you could even be using heroin.

What happens to drugs after they have their effect on your nervous system? Do they build up in the body to produce ever greater effects? Do they lurk in the tissues of the body and creep back at unsuspecting moments to produce memory loss, flashbacks, or mental disintegration? Most drugs are metabolized and out of the body within a few hours after they are administered. Any effects felt after that are the result of processes set in motion by the drugs, not of the drugs themselves. Two important exceptions are the fat-soluble chemicals in marijuana (THC) and PCP (phencyclidine). Substantial amounts of these chemicals remain in the fatty cells of the body and can be released into the blood later. The importance of this fact is in determining whether a drug has caused permanent damage. The presence of symptoms long after the fact does not mean that the drug is still present in your system unless you have taken large quantities of PCP or marijuana. Eventually also these chemicals are eliminated from the body.

Another factor to be aware of is the synergistic effect. This is the effect that put Karen Quinlan into a coma over 10 years ago. She took tranquilizers and alcohol at the same time, and the combination of the two drugs brought about the coma. There is a temptation to combine drugs to facilitate or amplify their effects. For instance, many people use alcohol to take the edge off the uncomfortable feelings of marijuana use. The result is a nearly comatose yet awake state—a blackout. Others like to mix barbiturates and alcohol to amplify the effect of the barbiturates. Speedballing is the alternating of amphetamines with either barbiturates or narcotics. It is definitely dangerous.

Dependency, Addiction, and Withdrawal

*T*he most commonly discussed factor in drug use is adaptation. The body adapts to the presence of the drug by increased tolerance, dependency, or addiction. Increased tolerance simply means that more of the drug is required to produce the effect. But an increased dosage raises the risk of negative side effects. Dependency is the psychological habituation of the drug effect. There is an interesting factor to dependency that is much discussed. That is denial. In order to persuade the user to continue using drugs even when the user knows better, the brain constructs a system of denial so that the user isn't aware of how bad the dependency really is. Everybody else can see how burnt out, dependent, and addicted the person is, but the user denies it. This denial continues until the dependency is so strong that the person finds it extremely hard to quit. The mind has by that time become dependent on the mood the drug creates.

Withdrawal from a drug is, therefore, always a painful process, even if the drug is just nicotine or caffeine. In many cases the user will experience an opposite effect during withdrawal, such as depression when quitting a stimulant like coffee or cigarettes. If an addiction is involved, that opposite effect can be extremely painful or deadly. And addiction is a physical dependency as well as a psychological dependency. Withdrawal from barbiturates and heroin can lead to death. Alcoholics Anonymous maintains that an alcoholic cannot "withdraw" from alcohol. He (she) can only abstain. The craving is still there.

What If You Are Using Drugs?

*I*t is a lot easier for a nonuser to decide not to use drugs than it is for a user to quit. What if you are using drugs and you would like to quit? For one thing, you are not alone. Ours is a heavily chemically dependent society, and most people don't like it that way. For that reason many treatment programs are available, and they are usually specialized for age groups.

But it is not easy to decide to get treatment, nor is it certain that the treatment will "take." You may know some young people who have been in and out of treatment centers and are still using drugs. One reason for this failure may be that religious concerns were not adequately dealt with. The Christian faith can help with chemical dependency.

Specifically, the Christian faith has two things to offer. It can provide the ultimate meaning and value you want in your life in order to be truly and genuinely yourself. If offers you what it takes to be authentic. It makes it possible for you truly to be yourself. Second, the Christian faith offers the strength of friendships to support you through the painful process of withdrawal and to guarantee its success.

The road of the Christian life is not an easy one. Christians are called to put aside their own pains and concerns and to concentrate their efforts on acts of love for their neighbors. This life of love is the satisfactory alternative to drug use that meets all of the conditions for an authentic life—that is, the life that will allow you to be yourself and will help you become the "somebody" you are destined to be. Most important, though, the Christian life is built to survive failure. No matter how badly you mess up your life, you can be forgiven and start all over again with a clean slate.

The fact that you may have used drugs does not prevent you from being a loving person in the fullest sense of the word. In fact, although this is not a reason to use drugs, the drug experience can make you more knowledgeable and hard-nosed about drug use, and the pain of withdrawal can make you more compassionate toward those trying to quit. This is called tough love, and it is often the exusers who best show this powerful quality.

So many drug users feel they have gone too far to be brought back. Their denial system fools them into thinking they really don't want to be brought back. Many of them feel they have done permanent damage to themselves and their lives. None of these people are likely to read this book until after they become chemically free. You may know some people like this. Their chief concern is that they have violated themselves. They feel certain there is no way they can be redeemed (brought back), so they pursue a path of self-destruction, getting ever more heavily into drugs and other self-destructive behaviors. In their own way they are trying to lead authentic lives. They are trying to be true to themselves as losers. Jesus did not die for only part of the problem. God did not sacrifice what was nearest and dearest to Himself merely to teach us the way.

Jesus died for our sins, and there is no sin too great for Him to cover. Moreover, He will be with us on the road back.

People who consider themselves to be unredeemable are really acting as their own judge, jury, and executioner. They are convicting, sentencing, and punishing themselves for their sins. God did away with that. He appointed Jesus as the Judge. Jesus is a serious Judge. He does not want us to throw our lives away. He wants us to be our true selves. But His sentence is mercy. Anyone who turns to Him for forgiveness will be forgiven.

God doesn't do it alone. He wants us to help Him accomplish His forgiveness. He wants us to be His agents in bringing the possibility of forgiveness to those who don't realize it is there. He wants us to minister to those who consider themselves unredeemable. When we do, we see miracles of love—amazing grace! I've talked to heroin junkies who have been turned totally around by Christ. I've talked to young people who were convinced they were goners with no way to go but down. They had, or thought they had, brain damage, psychosis, chronic alcoholism, mental disintegration, memory loss, or whatever. But they were brought back!

If you are in a youth group, it can be a supporting group for chemical users. (Members of my youth group regard themselves as the custodians of my coffee use, whether I like it or not!) That is what is meant by the Christian faith providing strength and support. It is not just the presence of Jesus that sustains people through hard times. It is also the presence of His people. In that way your youth group is a vital part of the whole church. It serves the function of ministry with youth within the church. So whether you need support to go the hard way like Mary Andrews, the rebel of the peer culture, or whether you need support to make difficult decisions about what paths to follow in life, or whether you need support to navigate the long and painful road back from your mistakes, it is a good idea to keep involved in your youth group. It is a precious thing.

*T*HINGS YOU CAN DO

Individual: If you are currently using drugs or alcohol, the best thing you could do for yourself is quit. Chances are you are not using an addictive drug, so you can probably quit on your own without a medical treatment program. You can begin by abstaining for one day. If your use is sporadic, pick a day when you would normally use the drug. For example, if you normally drink at parties, abstain at the next one. Don't try to quit all at once (cold turkey). Chances are you have some degree of dependency and won't be able to do it. Try several "practice" days. Then, when you are *sure* you can do it, try two days. The two most important ingredients in your quitting are your attitude and prayer. If you really want to quit, and since God is working with you, no one can keep you from stopping. You will still need a lot of patience. If your dependency is strong—for example, if you have been smoking for several years—it may take a long time to quit.

If your attempt doesn't work, don't despair. There is another resource you can call on—people. Your pastor is a good person to go to for help because his theology is nonjudgmental toward drug users. He understands that you can't go it alone and will pray with you and be there for support. He will also respond to what may seem to you a trivial concern, such as quitting cigarettes, because he won't consider that any better or worse than any other type of drug use. In addition, he may be able to gather together a few of your friends to work as a support group for you.

If you are not using drugs, try an experiment. As mentioned before, attitude is a prime factor in quitting. Choose a friend or family member who is using drugs, and try to influence his or her attitude to want to quit. Remember the denial system. You will have to plan your tactics very carefully. You might want to try the exercise in the group suggestions with your friend or family member.

Group: Invite a chemical dependency counselor or resource person to your group to provide information on chemical dependency. At your next meeting draw a profile of a person on the chalkboard or feltboard. Imagine that the profile is a drug user. (Don't specify the drug type.) Take turns writing or pinning one word descriptions of the drug user on the profile. Discuss what these words tell you about the self-image of a drug user.

Ethics clarification is an important tool in developing helpful attitudes toward drugs. You might want to use the following survey. One imaginative way to dramatize the survey results is to use different colored marbles or beans for yes and no and collect responses anonymously from each person for the whole group to see.

Drug Use Ethics Clarification

(Answer Yes or No)

1. The frequent use of alcohol is harmful to health.
2. The frequent use of marijuana is harmful to health.
3. The frequent use of prescribed tranquilizers, barbiturates, or stimulants is harmful to health.
4. The frequent use of marijuana is worse than the frequent use of alcohol.
5. The frequent use of marijuana is worse than the frequent use of prescribed drugs.
6. The decision to use marijuana should be up to the individual, like the use of alcohol is.
7. The prohibition of alcohol use by minors is a good law.
8. A good way to stop marijuana use is to spray it with dangerous pesticides.

7

Death and Suicide

*B*ill Jones just happened to go by Harold's room in their dormitory on his way to a Saturday night movie. Why not see if he wants to go with me, he thought. So he turned back and knocked, but there was no answer. Bill doesn't really know to this day why he tried the knob and, finding the door unlocked, opened it. But when he did, there was Harold hanging from the ceiling light fixture. He quickly jumped on the chair that Harold had kicked out from under him and untied the rope. Fortunately Harold was not dead.

By the time I got there, Harold was conscious and knew that his suicide attempt had failed. He was flailing his arms and legs as he lay on the bed in angry frustration. I tried to talk with him, but he was hysterical. "Why did you stop me?" he shrieked.

We took him to the hospital. There it was discovered that Harold had been deeply depressed over a series of disappointments, but no one had known how bad off he was. He could hardly remember what happened that day to make him want to take his life. Two weeks later he was a different person. "It's hard for me to believe I could do that," he said. "I guess I let myself get so down that I really was out of it. But I'm sure grateful that Bill Jones opened that door!"

I Our Paradoxical Approach to Death

*I*n view of the way people fight to stay alive, why would anyone want to kill himself or herself? We obviously have contradictory feelings about death. On the one hand, we fear it; it is what people

71

undoubtedly fear the most. How about you? What goes through your mind when you realize that you, like everyone else, some day will die?

The fear this thought engenders leads people in our society to act as though it won't happen to them. We avoid talking about it—even thinking about it. People who are dying of disease are seldom seen because they die in hospitals. Sometimes very few people visit them—and some who do would rather not.

On the other hand, we humans can be peculiarly attracted to death. The daredevil is one who likes to defy death by seeing how close he can come to it. As a culture we are attracted especially to violent death. We may not want to be around people who are dying from disease, but we like to see movies that portray violent death with all the gore. We seem fascinated by it. Hollywood knows that and, in order to make money, gives it to us. Suicidal desires show a similar fascination with death.

We see this same contradiction about death reflected in the natural world. On the one hand, all life is motivated to fight against death. Yet the energy of life is running down. This is the law of entropy you learn about in physics.

Christians, like others, have these contradictory feelings about death. In spite of your belief in eternal life, do you fear death? Most others do, including people of faith. Do you at times have an attraction to death—like to see violent movies, for example, or read about violent crimes? So do many others, including God's people. Have you at low periods in your life thought of death as a relief—an answer? So do a lot of other people, including those who believe in Christ.

What, then, makes the difference? We who believe have resources through our faith to deal with these thoughts and feelings. We have the Word of God, in which we can hear God speak His comforting and reassuring promises to us. We have recourse to prayer anytime we desire it. We can tell God about our fearful thoughts and troubled feelings. We have our church, where we worship and receive the inspiration and direction we need to make healthy decisions regarding our behavior. We have the "communion of saints," in which fellow Christians can be a support group to us like that of Alcoholics Anonymous. Also many churches in cooperative ventures are establishing emergency services such as suicide prevention centers.

Visions of Existence After Death

What scares us about death is that it seems so final. Have you seen the corpse of someone you knew lying in a casket? In our scientific age we ask an old question: "If a man die, shall he live again?" (Job 14:14). Modern secularists either say no or that there is no way of knowing. Positive answers usually come from religion.

Eastern religions teach an impersonal idea of immortality in which one's spirit becomes part of the cosmic spirit. Physicians Raymond Moody and Elizabeth Kuebler-Ross are convinced that some people in nearly dying have had experiences of "life after life" and then have recovered. These people no longer seem to fear death.

The Christian faith is unique in its vision of eternal life, since it proclaims a Savior who is resurrected from the dead. Because Jesus lives, we too shall live (John 14:19). It will not be only our spirit that lives, however, but our total person, including the body, as we confess in the Apostles' Creed, "I believe in the resurrection of the body and the life everlasting."

People who are suicidal have *no* vision of the future. This is not because they are secularists or atheists but because of their desperate state of mind.

Leading Cause of Death

Next to accidents, suicide is the leading cause of death among young people. When we consider that suicidal tendencies are probably involved in some accidents, suicide may well be at the top. Why would any young person with the probability of a long life ahead so fear the future that he or she would choose death instead?

Most people who commit suicide in our culture are in what to them is the intolerable pain of despair. In the distorted thinking that follows, they see the only answer to their hopelessness in death. Death appears also as the answer to their powerlessness. One power still remains—the power to take one's own life. If one still has this power, he or she is still a *somebody,* and in desperation it is more important to preserve one's identity as a somebody than to exist as a nobody. When a person's thinking becomes this distorted by the agony of despair, death begins to appear as light in the darkness—when actually it is the deeper darkness.

T   Suicide Preventing

hose who know from experience—like Harold—and those who have been devastated by the suicide of one whom they loved—like the authors of this book—can tell you loudly and clearly that suicide is no answer but rather a tragic end to answers. It is the destructive climax to believing one's own distorted delusions.

Yet suicide is a preventable tragedy. Since suicidal thoughts can enter the minds of any of us, the first step in prevention is doing what needs to be done when you become aware of the symptoms. If you are feeling miserable about yourself and hopeless about what lies ahead for you, you are probably turning in too much on yourself. The first thing to do is talk to somebody about how you feel. This will break into your isolation and interrupt the destructive monolog that you have been carrying on with yourself.

Suicide prevention centers are based on this principle. When you share your dark thoughts with others, you will also discover that they have felt at times like you do, even though in your loneliness you thought you were the only one. Talking with others brings the balance of objectivity into your otherwise subjectively distorted frame of mind. You are too close (subjective) to the situation to see it clearly. Sharing with others gives you a view from outside yourself (more objective) so that you see with better focus.

With whom can you talk? Often the people closest to you are the most likely to be overlooked and underrated. Our parents are a good example. They probably care more for us than anybody else, and yet we often assume that they won't understand. Give your parents the opportunity. They may be more helpful than you think. Sometimes an older brother or sister will be very understanding. Even though you may have withdrawn from your friends, reach out to them now, and you may be surprised how much they care. At least give your friends a chance.

I know it takes courage to do this. You wonder what they will think of you—or whether they will respond in a way that will make you wish you hadn't told them. But be patient with them. It may take a while for them to understand. Your first approach may catch them off guard so that they respond awkwardly. But they will recover from this. It also takes some people time to realize that you are serious, so you may have to mention it again.

Then there are your professional friends, one of whom is your pastor. Others include your school counselors. These people have been trained to be helpful to you in your troubles. Give them the opportunity.

God is your Friend. He may seem to be a million miles away, but He is really very close to you. In your low spirits you may think He doesn't care about you, but this is another example of how distorted our thinking can become when we isolate ourselves. God cared enough for us to send His Son to become one of us, and this Son has assured us that we are His friends (John 15:15).

Talk to Jesus in prayer, even if it seems that nobody is listening. He is—and it is good for you to tell Him how you feel, because He is your *Redeemer*. This means He will redeem your seemingly hopeless situation by bringing *real* light into your life to replace the delusionary light of suicide. He will answer your prayer. He may do so through the people with whom you choose to share your problem. Just as God reveals Himself in the flesh and blood of Jesus, so Jesus speaks to us through the flesh and blood of His people.

A Caring Group

We all need protection from our destructive tendencies as well as healing for our depressed spirits. Belonging to a group that cares about us can meet these needs. In the distant past there was little compassion for those who committed suicide. They were considered beyond God's grace. The fear of going to hell might have prevented some people from committing suicide as long as they were rational. But if their mental disturbance reached the point that they thought they were going to hell anyway, the fear of hell would no longer restrain them.

As we look back at that period in our history, we realize that God was probably the only one who really had compassion on such people and understood their pain. Today we realize that the suicidal person is not alone in his or her problem. All of us are involved to some extent. As St. Paul said, while each of us "will have to bear his own load" (Gal. 6:5), we are also to "bear one another's burdens" (Gal. 6:2). This is why, after a suicide, those who knew the person ask themselves what they did—or did not do—that may have contributed to the tragedy.

A senior girl in the high school in our neighborhood jumped from a bridge to her death after a school party. No one at the school, it seemed, had any idea of her despondency at the time, although afterwards some of the students recalled possible hints in the days preceding her death. Then they asked those awful questions: Could I have done something to have prevented this? Why didn't I follow up the clues and talk with her? Why didn't I pay more attention to her at the party when she seemed preoccupied? How could this happen to someone who seemed so much like us?

These are questions that need to be asked because the fault, if there is one, may be shared more than we would like to believe. For example, are you a person to whom someone in low spirits might come? Are you a person who is sensitive to others' feelings and listens well? If so, you would take such persons seriously and feel with them in their inner pain. You don't have to give advice—just be there. You encourage them by letting them know you care. Let them know that you believe that God cares, too.

The question goes even deeper. Are you aware when people withdraw into themselves? Can you sense that they are preoccupied with their own problems? The next is the hardest of all: Can you reach out to them by being friendly, encouraging them to talk and keeping in contact with them, even when in their depressed spirits they don't encourage you?

This may seem to be very hard, if not impossible, to do. If you know it is the right thing, you will have the confidence you need to do it. You are not betraying a confidence if you share with other responsible people your concern for the one who is hurting. The more people who know about the situation and who are sensitive and caring, the less likely that the depressed person will be able to withdraw.

Since belonging to a group in which the members care about each other is the best protection against our destructive tendencies, you also need to ask about the group to which you belong. Is it a caring community? Are people accepted by your group regardless of how "kooky" they may sound? Is your group good at listening for cries of help and also good at responding to those cries? Perhaps you think your group has a long way to go. I don't know of any group that doesn't have room for improvement. The more we see a group from the *inside*, the more aware we are of how far it has to go.

This gives your group something to work on. The ideal—which is always something beyond us—is what God had in mind for human community. Belonging to a group like this is also good preventative medicine for the mental distortions that can lead to suicide. The ounce of prevention, here as well as elsewhere, is worth a pound of cure.

Just as following good habits may keep your body healthy, so following similarly good habits for the mind and spirit tend to keep them healthy as well. These habits are chiefly the things that strengthen your faith in God. It is this faith that gives genuine light to your future and makes your life not only worth living, but an exciting challenge. The eternal life that we shall have after death begins now.

*T*HINGS YOU CAN DO

Individual: We rarely find the courage to talk to anybody about how we feel about death, and we just as rarely find anybody willing to talk with us on the subject. They either give some quick answer, religious or otherwise, that is supposed to end the discussion, or they try to distract the conversation by making a joke about death. Yet it is a subject that we need to talk about, so be persistent.

Pick an adult whom you respect for his or her honesty, and ask for this person's feelings about death. After responding to your question, he or she is likely to ask you about your thoughts and feelings—or at least ask why you asked. While it is true that we die alone, it is not true that we must deal with the subject of death alone. Facing the reality of our own death is a leap of faith that we can best make when we have shared our concern about it with others in God's family.

Group: Plan a program on the subject of suicide. Begin by giving each person the following quiz:

True or False.
1. People who talk about committing suicide don't do it.
2. Suicides happen without warning.
3. Suicidal people are fully intent on dying.
4. Once a person is suicidal, he or she is suicidal forever.
5. Improvement after a suicidal crisis means the suicidal risk is over.
6. Suicide is inherited or runs in the family.
7. There is no difference between men and women regarding suicide.
8. Suicide is one's own business, and others should not interfere.

9. People who may be thinking of suicide should be encouraged to talk about it.
10. People who take their life usually do so in an irrational state of mind.

While sitting in a circle, take up each question one at a time, allowing time for discussion of the answers. At the conclusion of the discussion, break up into groups of four, and brainstorm about how the group could be helpful to its members and others in their discouragements and possible suicidal thoughts. The small groups should then share their insights with the total group.

Answers:

1. *False.* In 8 out of 10 suicides the victims gave definite warnings of their intentions.
2. *False.* Studies reveal suicidal persons give many clues and warnings regarding their suicidal intentions.
3. *False.* Most suicidal people are undecided about living and dying and gamble with death, leaving others to save them.
4. *False.* One is suicidal for only a limited period of time.
5. *False.* Most suicides occur after a beginning improvement.
6. *False.* There is no genetic evidence for suicidal tendencies.
7. *False.* Men kill themselves more often than women, while women attempt suicide more often than men. As roles are changing in society, however, these statistics are also changing.
8. *False.* From a Christian point of view, what one does with one's own life is not just one's own business.
9. *True.* By talking about it, the suicidal person is likely to gain the needed objectivity to think more clearly.
10. *True.* The great majority of people in our western culture who commit suicide are in a despondent state of mind based on delusional threats that seem worse than death. On the other hand there are some people who, facing a fate they do not wish to endure, such as a medically incurable and debilitating illness, may in a rational frame of mind choose death. Two suicides mentioned in the Bible are related to this situation. Samson chose to die by bringing destruction on his enemies rather than being tortured to death by them. Saul chose to die by his own hand for the same reason. (Look up Judges 16:30 and 1 Sam. 31:4).

8

Pain, Grief, and Guilt

*T*he senior class at Gibson High was in a state of shock. Evelyn, a girl widely respected and liked, had been killed in an auto accident. After the funeral, which was attended by most of the class since classes for the day were canceled, the kids needed to talk.

Margie sought out the pastor of her church. She had been Evelyn's closest friend, and she was devastated by the loss. "Why?" she wanted to know. "Why does God allow such terrible things to happen?"

The pastor did not try to provide an answer. It was too important for Margie to cry it out. She was badly hurt because she lost a very dear friend. Her question was a protest. She was angry. Why should a 17-year-old girl like Evelyn have her life cut off when she had so much yet ahead of her?

Grieving Over What Is Lost

*M*argie's pain is the pain of grief. It comes when we lose someone or something very important to us. For Margie it was her friend. For others it may be the death of a father, mother, brother, or sister.

Although the protest is stated as a question at the moment of grief, it is really an expression of anger. The target of our anger is the kind of world in which we live. But who is responsible for this world? The most likely candidate is God. As Job said in his anger, "If it is not He [God], who then is it?" (Job 9:24). Why did God let it happen?

God understands our anger. He can take it. If we are thinking it, He wants us to say it. He knows we are not ready for an answer at the moment, but by expressing this question as a protest, we open the way for living positively with the question. As the grieving process continues, an answer of sorts begins to emerge.

But we need to ask this question before either we or our friends have had a significant loss. As the funeral liturgy says, "In the midst of life we are in death." This is a fallen world where sickness, accidents, war, and death are common events. Tragic and untimely deaths are the hardest of blows. God has never promised that we or our loved ones will be spared the calamities of life. But when such things happen, they are not to be seen as sent from God. A lot of things happen in this world that are not God's will, but He can *use* even what He does not *will.*

In other words, God can use the grief experience as a way of bringing about our personal growth as well as the growth of our relationships. This is His "Godness" in a fallen world. As mentioned in the previous chapter, I have experienced tragic and untimely death in my own family. From this experience I have discovered that sorrows like these can deepen our capacity for joy. This is because God is hidden in them and later reveals Himself.

What we can be sure of in the time of death is that God is with us and that He cares for us. His own Son was not spared death by crucifixion at the age of 33. He knows what it's like. Jesus wept with Mary and Martha at the death of their brother Lazarus, even though He knew He would bring Him back from the tomb. He wept because He was feeling their pain of grief. In His compassion He weeps with all those who suffer such significant losses.

The time is coming when "the kingdom of the world has become the kingdom of our Lord and of His Christ, and He shall reign for ever and ever" (Rev. 11:15). But in the meantime we have His understanding presence in this fallen world, even when we are angry with Him over our loss.

*I*t Other Losses

t is not only death that takes people away from us. You grieve if your parents separate and become divorced. Friendships also break up—sometimes with lots of pain. People who are going steady, for example, and who then break up, may grieve over the loss. Friends can move away. They can also lose interest in the friendship. I remember the pain I felt after a good friend who was older than I went to college. When he returned for vacations, he was no longer interested in our friendship.

Although we may be angry over the loss, the predominant feeling is sadness—sorrow. Because the loss seems so permanent we wonder whether we will ever be happy again. Grief also saps our energy. We wonder if we will ever again feel enthusiastic about living.

Guilt: Take Only Your Share

*O*ur grief is often complicated by the pain of guilt. What did I do wrong to lose my friend, parent, or sister? Margie finally got to this in her talk with her pastor. "We had a quarrel the day before the accident," she said. "I see now how petty I was. She liked to tease. She laughed at my new haircut—said it looked like I'd been out in the wind—and I got irritated."

"How did you show it?" the pastor asked. He was helping her to talk about it.

"I told her that her hair didn't look so hot either. She was hurt by that and said she was only kidding. But I was still mad, and we didn't talk much the rest of the day—and now she's gone."

When we feel guilty, we feel judged, but who is judging us— God? We think so at the time. A more likely answer is that we are judging ourselves. Margie could almost believe that she lost her friend as a punishment for the quarrel. Such feelings of guilt add to the pain of loss and may even be the hardest to bear.

Our guilt at these times can be irrational. For example, when Tom's parents were divorced, Tom believed it was his fault. "I made my dad go away," he said. Tom and his dad had a lot of father-son conflicts, but Tom didn't cause him to leave. His dad had other reasons for leaving.

Why do grieving people blame themselves? Don't we usually do the opposite? We often resist taking any blame and instead blame others. I imagine Margie blamed Evelyn at the time of the quarrel, and Tom blamed his dad for their fights. They both must have had some guilt at the time, but it didn't show. When the loss happens, however, it is like a judgment on us, and our hidden guilt takes over. Now we can be just as irrational by taking all of the blame on ourselves as we were when we blamed it all on the other.

Placing the blame on the other and taking the blame on ourselves are opposite sides of the same coin, and the coin is our tendency to be self-centered. What Margie and Tom and others like them need to do is to take their share of responsibility but not more

81

than their share. Responsibilities are widely spread, as we saw in the previous chapter on suicide.

The only answer to the guilt in our grief, once we have taken our share and not the whole load, is not punishment but forgiveness. It is the same Good News we've talked about before. God forgives us in Christ. Let it happen. Instead of letting forgiveness happen, however, we would rather go back in time, live the difficult situation over, do our part differently. But with death we can't, so the only way to go forward is to let the past be forgiven.

If this should be your situation, you may have to confess your guilt to a trusted friend, as you would to God. The forgiveness of God then works its way in your soul, and you can forgive yourself.

*G*rieving Is Healing

*G*rieving is a natural process of healing when we have been hurt by a significant loss. It's hard to realize this at the time—not only if you are the griever, but also when it is someone else whom you know. Since grieving hurts, how can it be healing? In feeling our grief, we seem to be adding to the hurt.

Grieving is inescapable when the loss is severe. Our hurt throbs just like it would if our wound were physical. The way of healing is to feel the pain and to share how it feels with others. If we run from it and try to distract ourselves in all kinds of activities and/or put up a happy front, the wound remains unhealed just below the surface. It may even become infected.

When I was pastoral counselor at a church college, I encountered this delayed grief among students who had lost a parent, usually during their teenage years. They would ask to see me about some current problem, usually about study difficulties, but before we were finished, the old wound began to show. The subject usually came up when I inquired about the student's family. After telling me a few interesting facts, the student said something like "My father died when I was a sophomore in high school."

When I asked the student to tell me about it, tears would come to the eyes, and soon the student was sobbing as though the death had occurred only yesterday. When I inquired whether the student had ever shared this feeling about the death with anybody at the time, the answer was almost always no. There had been no healthy grieving, probably because people thought 16-year-olds didn't need a shoulder to cry on. So now three or four years later the delayed grief showed up in other problems. It won't go away until the pain is shared, often repeatedly, with others. Beneath the surface of those whose grieving has been delayed is a sadness and a loneliness that disrupts concentration. It is no wonder that one's studies are affected.

Healthy Grieving

*I*t is important for those who have experienced loss to face the pain when it happens and share their feelings with others who care. Some, however, may not want to listen. It makes them uncomfortable to hear about another's sadness and pain, so they quickly try to cheer the other up, or they change the subject.

If this should happen to you when you are trying to express your grief, don't let it discourage you from talking to someone else. Unfortunately, many people do not seem to understand that talking about grief is the way that pain is relieved. They try to get the other's mind off the loss, as though this were possible, and, without realizing it, they do just the opposite of what they should do.

Boys in particular tend to laugh off the dejection of a friend who feels bad because a girl has broken off with him or has not responded to his interest. "Girls are like buses—another will soon be along," they say, "so forget it!" Males in our culture tend to have difficulty acknowledging their pain or grief—or for that matter, acknowledging any vulnerability. Females are more liberated and can not only admit their sorrow but also weep openly.

So if it is your friends who are grieving rather than you, be a good listener. Tell them you are sorry to hear that their mother, father, sister, or brother has died or that their parents are getting a divorce or that their steady relationship has broken up. Usually they will express appreciation of this. That is your opportunity to draw them out on how they are getting along. Try to feel with them in their sense of loss, and don't hesitate to tell them of these feelings.

They may not say much when you first give them the opportunity, especially males, but the second or third time you inquire about how "things are going." they may share more of their sadness. After the initial shock, the waves of grief often hit again three and six months after the event and even a year later. Keep tabs on your grieving friends. It is important to believe that simply sharing their grief is healing. Otherwise you may get discouraged when people don't respond right away to your offer to talk with them.

Some do not know what is good for them when they are in pain. It is up to their friends to provide them with the kind of care they need, even if they have to be persistent in their efforts.

I Healing Happens

f you are grieving for someone dear like Margie is, follow the ways for healthy grieving described in this chapter. As you do, you will notice as time goes on that your grief is lessening. Time alone does not heal, but time plus healthy grieving does. When this happens, let your grief go. Don't hold on to it. Some people do—probably because they have grown accustomed to feeling sad. Enthusiasm for living *does* return. It is part of the newness of life that we have in Jesus Christ. It is life with a capital *L*.

You may never get a rational understanding of why your friend, father, mother, or sibling died, but you will be able to live positively anyhow because you know that God is with you even as He is with the one who died. Your confidence in Him will permit you to wait until "the life everlasting" when we "shall understand fully" (1 Cor. 13:12).

If your situation is like Tom's, you may not understand why your folks couldn't stay together. Your grief over the divorce, like others' grief over broken romances and other friendships, will heal. You will be able to live with the brokenness. You will realize through God's caring presence that broken relationships do not have to break *you*. God can use even this brokenness for your growth in wholeness.

You still have living parents, though one may not be accessible at the present. Since we do not know what the future may bring, do your best to remain open to both parents. The parent to whom you have the least access probably has suffered also. Dare to hope—and to pray—for good things yet to come in these relationships.

The age to come has in one sense already come. The fresh start God gives is like a resurrection. As your grief heals, life opens to you again. Your loved one is still dear to you, but now you can let him or her die. You take the pleasant memories of this relationship with you to bless your other relationships. The unpleasant memories are forgiven; God will use them for your growth. Jesus said, "I am the Way and the Truth and the Life" (John 14:6). He is each one of these for you in a very special way in your sorrow.

*T*HINGS YOU CAN DO

Individual: Take advantage of any opportunity you have to listen as friends talk about their experience of a loss, such as that of a grandparent. Ask your parents about deaths they experienced in their families—how old they were at the time, what it felt like, and how long it took for those feelings to go away.

If a friend breaks up with a boyfriend or girlfriend and feels bad about it, be a good listener even though the same laments are repeated many times. People often relive the events preceding a breakup just as they do the events preceding a death. They are trying to come to some kind of peace over the loss so that it can heal.

Group: Each person in the group takes a few minutes to make a list of the losses in his or her life. These would include family members such as grandparents who have died or even pets when the loss has been deeply felt. They would also include relationships broken by causes other than death unless they feel too embarrassed to mention them.

Then each lists the feelings experienced over these losses and tries to distinguish between the various feelings. They should be described with analogies and metaphors such as "Feeling sad is like having something heavy inside my chest."

When all are finished, the group divides into threes, and each person takes a turn in sharing one loss from their list, after which the other two may ask clarifying questions in an attempt to understand better.

9

The Future and Faith

What Is Faith?

*T*hroughout this book, in relating to various concerns of teen-agers, we have made statements of faith as if they were central to our understanding of the issues. For persons of religious persuasion, faith informs their understanding on almost every issue.

Perhaps you will think it is narrow-minded to look first to your faith when there are important issues that concern you, particularly if you are not sure of your faith. When I was a teenager, I was by no means sure of my faith. It seemed as if the church was always telling me what to think—not letting me make my own decisions in the vast marketplace of the world. It seemed to me that a more worldly and scientific way of looking at issues was more intelligent. I didn't know whether the teachings of the church could stand up to the tests of the "real world." For me the possibility existed that the church prescribed its own morals to protect its own interests and that the faithful churchgoers just might be "phonies." It was not without testing and struggling that I have come to see my life through the eyes of faith.

Faith cannot live without doubt, and you will probably feel it necessary to live out many of your doubts. Unfortunately, many people hurt themselves unnecessarily in acting out their doubts about God. Please consider the option of faith before you throw your life away in doubt.

Margaret

*M*argaret is a young black youth worker in an inner city youth ministry. Although she is young (a recent college graduate), her faith commitment is strong. I marveled at the level of her commitment and at the maturity of her faith as I watched her work. What was there about her that seemed so genuine, so likable?

Margaret didn't run around trying to convert kids to Christianity as some zealous inner-city youth workers do—as if that will solve all of their problems. In fact, she didn't seem concerned with that at all. She just naturally enjoyed herself and her work with young people, and they all loved her.

One Sunday, Margaret was a guest speaker at our church. She spoke only about five minutes, but what she said had a profound impact on me and others in my church.

Margaret told how she had come to faith. She was raised in a religious home—as many of us are—but was not quite sure of her own commitment to that religion. What Margaret found objectionable was that her church did not confront racism. Being black, Margaret often felt the pains of discrimination, and she developed a fierce desire to overcome the obstacles that it presented. She didn't feel enough support from her church. It seemed to ignore the issue, always avoiding public confrontations with racism. It seemed to be more concerned with issues of personal morality and the afterlife. Margaret wanted to "be somebody," and if she had to go outside of the church to do that, that was what she would do.

One day when Margaret was a senior in high school, a friend of hers was gunned down by mistake by a white policeman. She felt intense hatred for that policeman—indeed, for all white people. How could she, a black woman, ever gain enough respect in society to "be somebody." Just when she might be getting somewhere, she could just be gunned down by mistake because "they all look alike." It seemed as if there were no option but to hate the white people.

But that just didn't sit right with her. Her church had taught her to love not only black folks or the nice white folks, but even her enemies. Although Margaret wasn't about to forgive that white policeman, she had to admit that it wasn't right to hate all the white people. Such thoughts made her feel guilty and made her wonder if she was much better than the policeman. Maybe he simply made an honest mistake. Maybe he didn't even hate black people. But Margaret knew her hatred was real, and that is where her struggle for faith began. How could she find meaning for her life in this crazy, mixed-up, hostile world of which she was an active part?

Margaret didn't give us any more details of the struggle, but there she was, full of self-respect, full of love, and full of confidence in her own ability to live and enjoy life.

The Surprising Future of the Hidden God

*F*or every faithful person, there is a story of a struggle with that faith. I could have told you mine, and you could perhaps tell your own. More likely, you are either just beginning to question your faith or are involved in the struggle yourself. This is perhaps the most important issue teenagers can discuss—the issue of faith. Struggling with faith and doubt, searching for meaning in life, seeking confidence for the future, and finding self-acceptance are all vital elements of the process of becoming yourself, which is the teenage process of developing identity.

Do you ever feel terrified or uneasy about the future? If you don't, you are unusual. There is much to worry about these days, from atomic bombs to environmental pollution to unemployment. This uneasiness about the future is fueled by our society's human-centered vision of the future. We project what we think the future could be, based on what we know now, and sometimes that is pessimistic because we feel so bad about ourselves that we don't really want the future to happen at all.

But there is another future! That is God's future, and the thing that most marks God's future is that it surprises people. "My thoughts are not your thoughts, neither are your ways My ways, says the Lord" (Is. 55:8). You can never predict what He is going to do next. We celebrate His two most surprising acts at Christmas and Easter. At Christmas we celebrate the entrance of God into the world—in a Baby born in a barn. At Easter we celebrate the victory of the resurrection—a surprising act indeed. In our day He continues to act. God still has control of history. Though you might fear total nuclear destruction or some other end of the world, God still has the power to prevent the buttons from being pushed.

The Rogues Gallery

*O*ne of the interesting twists in the Bible that shows how surprising God's actions in history are is the "rogues gallery." * Have you

---

* John Drury, *Tradition and Design in Luke's Gospel* (Atlanta: John Knox Press, 1976) p. 78.

ever given a thought to the morality of some of the Bible heroes? Jacob was a rascal if there ever was one. He stole his brother's inheritance. His uncle Laban was wily and tricked him into marrying his ugly daughter, but Jacob got the upper hand in the end by craftily extorting most of his uncle's livestock. Then there was King David. He killed Bathsheba's husband so he could marry her. These are the characters through whom God worked out His history of salvation. Obviously, we would never sanction the killing of a man to get his wife, but it is comforting to know that God's future doesn't depend on our morality. Yet we know we should try to be honest, good, trustworthy, and loving people.

Jesus often told stories that illustrated the surprising way in which God acts. Most of you have heard at least some of these parables, like that of the Prodigal Son and the Good Samaritan. One little-known but very surprising story is that of the Dishonest Steward (Luke 16:1-8).

Jesus said to His disciples,

> "There was a rich man who had a steward, and charges were brought to him that this man was wasting his goods. And he called him and said to him, 'What is this that I hear about you? Turn in the account of your stewardship, for you can no longer be steward.' And the steward said to himself, 'What shall I do, since my master is taking the stewardship away from me? I am not strong enough to dig, and I am ashamed to beg. I have decided what to do, so that people may receive me into their houses when I am put out of the stewardship.' So, summoning his master's debtors one by one, he said to the first, 'How much do you owe my master?' He said, 'A hundred measures of oil.' And he said to him, 'Take your bill, and sit down quickly and write fifty.' Then he said to another, 'And how much do you owe?' He said, 'A hundred measures of wheat.' He said to him, 'Take your bill, and write eighty.'

At this point, we would expect the dishonest steward to get caught and be punished for his dishonesty. But Jesus concluded the story, "The master commended the dishonest steward for his prudence."

"The Pharisees, who were lovers of money, heard all this, and they scoffed at Jesus" (Luke 16:14). There is some kind of justice in Jesus' surprising sympathy for the dishonest steward. He did not commend his dishonesty; the rich master did. But the Pharisees, who were the rich masters, scoffed at the story. There were no rich masters who forgave like the one in Jesus' story. So Jesus pointed out how different are the ways of God from those of human beings. "You are those who justify yourselves before men, but God knows your hearts; for what is considered important among men is an abomination in the sight of God" (Luke 16:15). We can be grateful it is God's history that is happening and not our own.

*H*ow   You

*H*ow do you fit into God's future? One question that many people ask is how God can have time to be personally concerned about each individual person who has ever lived. Some people, in fact, never pray for anything for themselves because they do not want to take God's time away from somebody else. However, that is our limited human way of looking at things. The invention of the computer has made this dilemma easier to resolve. We can readily imagine God to have a memory bank complex enough to deal with the situation. He has a program with which He can keep track of each individual person who has ever lived. As we mentioned before, He wants each person to achieve wholeness of mind, body, and spirit, and at any one time you are at some stage on the path toward the self you are to become.

We are endowed with a consciousness that allows us to live in the present and look forward to the future with confidence that it will unfold according to God's will. But that's easier said than done. Who doesn't ever get down on himself or herself for the way things are? Who doesn't ever become discouraged at the prospects of the future?

We are too limited by our human way of looking at things. God accepts us the way we are and has His own vision of who we are to become. It might look to you as if there isn't enough freedom in God's plan. His plan acknowledges human limitations and evil and maximizes our freedom.

On the other hand, maybe you feel there is too much freedom in God's plan, at least in the way I am describing it. God's unconditional acceptance doesn't mean we have His approval to do whatever we choose. It means that much is expected of us. Yet we won't think or behave as is best, and we will deviate from the desired program. But remember the "rogues gallery." God pursues His vision through our waywardness. This is another problem young people experience in the struggle for faith. How can we ever get back on track once we've gotten too far off?

Throughout this book, we have been stressing the religious and psychological value of forgiveness. It is absolutely necessary for you to move into the future. You have to be able to start over, no matter how far you have strayed from your true self. God didn't ask us if we were ready for Jesus. He didn't make the early Christians crawl around on their knees begging for forgiveness. He just did it—He gave His Son for our sins. That means Jesus died for all of our sins, and there are none too great to be forgiven. The future opens when we can let God love us—when we can accept his forgiveness. Then we are on track with God's future.

No matter how many times we hear it, however, we find it hard to let God forgive us that easily. Sometimes it helps to say we're sorry to people we've hurt or offended, but God doesn't really need that. If He had to wait until we did the right thing or felt good about ourselves, our lives would be over. Heaven can't wait.

The big worry we have about God's unconditional forgiveness is that it will encourage everybody to do awful things. If not that, then at least no one will try for a better world. But isn't that already the way it is in the human vision of the future? Doesn't competition and a "me first" attitude already dictate what happens in our world, whether in the sophisticated working of business or in the crude workings of the street? Everybody is naturally selfish, and unconditional forgiveness doesn't make us any more selfish. If we know we are forgiven, we can be freed up to try to make this a better world. Maybe God's ways aren't so hidden and mysterious after all if we can only believe in forgiveness—that is, if we can only believe in Jesus.

Evil and Suffering

*I*f God's future is so desirable and so easy to get at, and if faith is so simple, then why is there a human distortion of the future, and why is there doubt? One thing to realize is that it is much harder for us to believe than it was for Christians of the first 15 centuries. That is because we have been educated in a scientific world view. To many young people, for example, it looks as if medicine is doing a much better job than religion when it comes to human suffering. In fact, that is perhaps the hardest question that can be asked in this issue of faith: How can a loving God allow all of this suffering in the world? How can God be good and allow such unfairness? And what about evil? No wonder we doubt.

These questions are ancient. Listen to the doubts of Job: "The night racks my bones, and the pain that gnaws me takes no rest. . . . I cry to Thee and Thou dost not answer me" (Job 30:17, 20a). Or hear the doubts of Jeremiah when Jerusalem was destroyed by the Babylonians after a long siege during which the people ate their own children for lack of other food: "Look, O Lord, and see! With whom [else] hast Thou dealt thus? Should women eat their offspring, the children of their tender care?" (Lam. 2:20a). The disciples also wondered about suffering: "Rabbi, who sinned, this man or his parents, that he was born blind?" (John 9:2b).

It is easy for religious persons to make some statement of faith as an easy answer to the question of suffering and evil. Listen to the words of Job's friend, Eliphaz: "Behold, happy is the man whom God reproves; therefore despise not the chastening of the Almighty" (Job 5:17).

When one is really sensitive or really suffering, such trite statements of faith do no good. One has to really know. Our doubts make us put God to the test—and that is okay. God can stand that. When Job put God to the test, he discovered something remarkable. When Margaret put God to the test, she discovered something remarkable. It was out of this discovery that they both came to faith.

What Job and Margaret discovered was that they were far from perfect. They came to realize that they were a big part of the problem. They asked God to forgive them and readily accepted the forgiveness that He offered. Then the future was opened for them.

In the Job story, even though it was the devil's mischief that started all the trouble for Job, it was Job's confession that he was a big part of the problem and needed forgiveness that was the key to his future. That was the point at which he started over.

If your faith can deal with the questions of evil and suffering, then it will probably work for you. It will not be a cheap, counterfeit solution to life's problems, nor will it be an impotent solution to the most profound and evil suffering. Science can ask the questions—Where is God? How can life go on after death?—but it cannot answer them—at least not yet. The big question that faith answers is "Who will go with me through life, through death, and beyond?"

O Sick Religion

*O*ne of the difficulties I encounter with my human vision is that I always want to be complete, to "be there," to have it all together now. It takes courage to admit that we will not make it in our lifetime.

We have to pass through the gate of death. It is too easy to get smug and complacent about our faith. There are many expressions of this smugness and complacency. One is cheap grace, which leads us to feel it isn't even necessary to try to change things in the world. More often the problem is moralism or legalism; we decide that by virtue of our exemplary religious faith, we are better than other people. Jesus issued many warnings against "sick" religion. "Woe to you Pharisees! for you love the best seat in the synagogues and salutations in the market place" (Luke 11:43).

The best antidote for "sick religion" is to admit your doubts and questions openly and bring them before God. It is all right to question Him. His love is unconditional, and He wants you to be honest with Him. Asking why gives Him the opportunity to give you an answer and build your faith. He has even given you the radical freedom to turn your back on Him and reject His offer of forgiveness, but when you do that, you have passed beyond doubt to a decision. Even if that happens in your life, He is always ready to receive you back; He has made a commitment to you in your baptism. St. Paul had decided against God. He held the coats for the thugs who stoned Christians. Jesus stopped him dead in his tracks on the road to Damascus and made him a believer—*amazing grace!*

The song "Amazing Grace" was written by a once cruel and greedy slave trader who was saved by no actions or desire of his own. But don't emphasize your doubts, expecting God to act in your life the way He did in Paul's. He doesn't want us to suffer from doubts; He wants to overcome them. In times of doubt and temptation, remember the words of a distraught father: "I believe; help my unbelief!" (Mark 9:24).

*T*HINGS YOU CAN DO

Individual: Many visions of the future are presented in popular movies, books, and television shows. Some of these visions have religious significance, but few, if any, have first-hand Christian significance. Some are allegories of Christian vision, such as *Lord of the Rings* and the *Tales of Narnia*. Others have interesting parallels, such as *Star Wars* and *The Empire Strikes Back*. Some take the basic Christian mystery of resurrection and build a story around that; an example is *ET*. However, none of these actually include Christ in their visions of the future.

What vision of the future do you have? Knowing what you do about Jesus and faith, what vision of the future do you project? Write a religious science fiction story of the future that is as true to the Bible and faith as it is to scientific projections. Share it with your pastor, youth leader, or someone else you trust with religious feelings and thought.

Group: Stage a public forum or debate in your youth group or with another group in your community on the subject of the future. Some possible topics might be

1. What are the apocalyptic social and political conditions in our world today? The word *apocalyptic* means judgment and destruction as in the movie *Apocalypse Now.*
2. What is the future of religion in a technological world?
3. What will be the major changes in society or living conditions within the next five years?
4. What is the Biblical picture of the future—of the end of the world?

10

The New Age
and the Church

Brad

*B*rad quit going to church when he was a junior in high school. He would have quit earlier, but he felt guilty about not going, so he kept going sporadically through his sophomore year even though he wasn't interested. Brad's pastor was surprised to find Brad no longer going to church, but he couldn't do anything about it. He was so surprised because Brad had been one of the most active youth in the junior high group. In junior high school Brad was involved in about every activity possible at the church from choir to confirmation to activities club. He seemed to find the meaning and center for his life at the church. Then two years later he dropped out.

What happened in those two years was this: Brad went out for football when he was a sophomore. The coach was an extremely kind, yet strict, man. He built his team on discipline and team spirit. The players spent as much time together off the field as they did on. The coach made sure there were plenty of opportunities for being together in fun and meaningful ways, both during the season and after. The coach did not promote all these activities only because he wanted the team to win. He also just liked to see young men have a good time in "clean" fun.

And the team won. The coach didn't require them to win, but he did take great pains to make sure each player felt respected and was treated fairly, on the field and off, by coaches and players alike.

Soon Brad wanted to be with his teammates more than with his friends at church. It was on the team that he felt love, respect, and a sense of fairness. He really felt he belonged. It was not that love, respect, and fairness were not to be found at church or that he didn't feel he belonged there. On the contrary, that was why he found so much enjoyment there during junior high. Now he felt a little guilty about not going, but he couldn't find time for both. The team experience was so intense that it just beat out the church experience—for a while.

*I*n the creed we call the church the "communion of saints." In this

What Is Community?

understanding the church is a unique community—a community of believers in Jesus Christ. There are many other ways to think about the church, such as a building on a certain corner, but thinking about it as a community says so much more. It points to the people who go there and what they have in common.

Where would you expect to find a community? Ordinarily, people think of a community as a place where they can find love. In a community, people have some degree of respect for one another and their rights. There has to be some sense of fairness about things, or you'd not tolerate living there. There is a feeling of *belonging*, a feeling of being "somebody." This is a kind of community Brad found, first at his church and later in high school athletics. Do you feel that you are part of a community?

You might not feel you belong to any community. That isn't so unusual in our society today. Many of the values we live by work against community. For instance, we are encouraged to be more concerned about our rights than about the welfare of other people in our community. In some societies, though very few, the welfare of others comes first.

Many of the institutions in our society in which you might hope to find some love, respect, and justice just don't have them. The place where that hurts most is in the family. If you don't feel you belong to a family that has love, respect, and fairness, you know how painful it is. For those who love the church, it is equally painful to realize that not all churches measure up to the requirements of community, either.

This was not the case with Brad's church. To him it seemed like a community. He felt a sense of belonging in his church. But his football team was also a community. There, too, he felt he belonged.

T Longing for Belonging

he longing for belonging is a desire for fulfillment. It is part of the quest for your true identity. It is the quest for authenticity—the search for meaning. In order to be somebody, you have to know not only *who* you are, but *Whose* you are.

As we said in the last chapter, faith satisfies this need, but many people deprive themselves of the full benefit of faith, that of belonging to a church. For many, community is found, to some extent, somewhere else. Then faith becomes a private affair. Can faith and the church be separated like that? In order to deal with this problem we have to look at what the church *really* is.

W What Is the Church?

hat *is* the church? If you haven't ever thought much about this question, you may be pleasantly surprised to find out what it is. We have already said that the church is the community of believers. The big question that comes up is, if the church is the community of believers, why do some church people act like they don't believe? How can some people go to church all nice and polite and then go out in their everyday lives and act just the opposite?

Well, we first have to ask ourselves, "Are we any better?" I remember when I was younger, I brought the issue of the Vietnam War to my church. When the members did not respond to my proposals for peace, I angrily quit the church. Assuming, incorrectly, that all churches were alike, I quit going to church altogether for several years. Now I know, like Margaret in the last chapter, that I am not so much better. Now that I am older and have a little more power to change things, I often don't do anything, because I'm too busy doing what I want. We have to ask ourselves, "Are we any better?"

Why do we expect church people to be morally better than the average person? Jews go to synagogs, football players play on their teams, and Christians go to church. None of these communities is perfect. They all contain opportunists, that is, people who are in it only for their own gain. They all contain hypocrites, that is, people who claim to be morally superior, but do immoral things. Why expect any more of the church than of any other organization?

The reason we expect more of the church is that the church has a higher purpose. There are a lot of organizations with good people in them, but the church *alone* was, and still is, called out by Christ to be the means through which God will complete His work of reconciling the world to Himself (2 Cor. 5:18-19). This means that in Christ God started something that would save the whole world from self-destruction and bring it back into His love. That something is forgiveness, and the church is carrying out what Christ started by calling others to believe in Him. In that sense Christians are "ambassadors" for Christ, and the church will continue with this work until He returns.

We can't say that a football team has this high calling. We expect it to provide purpose, entertainment, recreation, commitment, etc., but we don't expect it to reconcile the world to God! Probably the institution that comes the closest to providing that kind of ultimate purpose is the family. But Jesus told us that His family, that is, "whoever does the will of God" (Mark 3:35), supersedes our earthly families. In other words we are called to leave behind our family allegiances to become members of the eternal family of God. This is the high calling of the church, so we just can't say that the church is a fallible institution and leave it at that.

As you can probably see, a big part of the question, What is the church? boils down to, Who is a "true" Christian and who isn't? How can anyone answer this question?

The early church was faced with the same question. For instance, the Galatians tried to use the commandments and good works to prove who was a true believer. In this situation Paul reacted very strongly. He said that it is faith and faith only that makes us acceptable to God because faith grasps Christ. Following the commandments and doing good works are important, but that is not what justifies us.

On a recent visit to Central America a young American was overwhelmed by the suffering of the homeless children there. She said to me, "How can I justify my existence in the face of all this poverty and suffering? My American life-style even contributes to their condition, and there is nothing I can do for them. All I can do is pray that God forgives me." Christ has done that for those who believe in Him.

The Invisible Church

When the Romans began to persecute the early church, it became a little easier to tell who was a true believer and who wasn't, at least externally. It became easier to tell because most, but not all, of the opportunists quit. It simply wasn't worth suffering for whatever advantage belonging to the church offered. During times of persecution most of the Christians were genuine, because the threat of torture and death was a strong incentive to leave the church.

During these times they developed an underground church in which they recognized each other with secret signs and symbols. They were a church "invisible" to society. Of course, the authorities knew they were there. In fact, it was convenient to blame them for all sorts of troubles in society. They were considered to be subversives. The Roman emperor Nero blamed them for burning down Rome. In reality, he was suspected of having torched the city himself for an urban renewal project!

After a period of persecution, a lot of Christians wanted to get back into the church. Of course, the Christians who endured the persecutions resented these "fair-weather" saints. At first they didn't want to accept them, but for the most part they finally forgave them and let them back in. When the church became legal in A.D. 313, one group, the Donatists of North Africa, seceded from the church over this issue.

After the emperor Constantine legalized Christianity, there was no underground church. But the invisible aspect of the underground church continued to exist above ground. God, and only God, knows who truly believes and who doesn't. So the true church of true believers remains invisible to the human eye.

Of course, after Christianity became legal, all sorts of people joined—for all sorts of reasons. After all, the emperor himself was a Christian. What better way to come up in the world! The presence of so many obviously insincere Christians prompted the church leaders (bishops) to propose minimum standards for being a Christian. Pretty soon they were up to their elbows in rules, regulations, and politics.

The bishops were trying to keep the church unified (catholic) and visible. They wanted to be able to say, "The catholic church is the one true church. Everyone in it is genuine and saved. Everyone not in it is untrue and damned." This effort more or less worked for over 1,000 years. However, in that time some highly questionable practices arose to guarantee the genuineness of faith. Salvation was bought and sold by the church; kings, emperors, governors, and all other rulers were required to submit to the authority of the pope, the cardinals, and the bishops; and everyone was required to contribute heavily to the church.

Some Christians questioned this logic. They questioned the authority of the leaders of the church to make all these requirements. The church leaders had a nifty little answer to this question. They said that Scripture and tradition were the authority for their actions. The only catch was that they *were* the tradition, and the pope was the guardian of it. His proclamations were unquestioned. Also, the Bible was written in Latin. Even if it had been written in the language the people spoke, there were no printing presses, and most of the people couldn't read.

*S*ince the civil rights movement   The Protestant Reformation

Since the civil rights movement and the Vietnam War, we are familiar with the idea of protest. Of course, there were protesters of the practices and power of the Roman Catholic Church. However, they were burned at the stake—men and women like John Huss, Wycliffe, and Joan of Arc.

Martin Luther was the primary person behind the protest reform movement in the Catholic Church. In his 95 Theses he condemned the practice of buying and selling forgiveness of sins (indulgences). He didn't break away from the Roman Catholic Church—it excommunicated him and probably would have killed him had he not been rescued by the ruler of Saxony. While he was in hiding in the Wartburg Castle, Luther developed his religious understanding and translated the New Testament into German so everybody could read it. The timing was perfect, because the printing press had only recently been developed in the same country.

Soon other reformers broke away from the Catholic Church—Calvinists (later Presbyterians), the Church of England (Episcopalians), and others. Later, other churches split off from these. The Puritans are an example of a Calvinist spin-off. Their theology highly influenced the form of government and lifestyle we have in the United States.

Many of these splits resulted in wars, but finally the Catholic Church itself reformed, though not to the point where it could reconcile with the Protestant churches. By that time the differences were too great. Luther had started a whole new revolution in thought, and even the Protestant churches are as yet unable to resolve their differences.

The Mysterious Body of Christ

*T*oday we have hundreds of churches, each with its own doctrine and a mixture of true believers and pretenders. Only God knows for sure who is who. Yet there is a real and universal (catholic) church. It is a church invisible to our eyes, because we can't be sure who is in it and who is not.

We have just described a mystery—something that is real, but invisible. That's the way it has to be. Otherwise, human eyes would be judging human hearts, and that's an inaccurate procedure even in the courtroom. This mystery has been described in another way. The invisible church has been called the body of Christ. Each individual believer is a member of the body (1 Cor. 12:12). Being a member is the ultimate in belonging. This mystical understanding of the church emphasizes again *Whose* we are.

But our modern world does not put much faith in supernatural, invisible, or mystical entities. Do you really want to belong to an organization that has its ultimate meaning only in some invisible sense?

Sometimes the fruits of the invisible church will show up in places outside of the visible church, like on Brad's football team. Sometimes the invisible church shows its influence in a labor union, or a service organization, or on a job site. At key positions in these organizations you will often find committed Christians working to establish conditions of love and justice. Such was the case on Brad's football team.

The Marks of the Church

*S*o what is the point of having churches? Why not tear them all down and build social service agencies? Isn't the visible church just like any other organization that tries to do good? After all, the real church is invisible—spiritual. Isn't the visible church just another place where the love of God shows itself in the world? Unfortunately, that is the way many people look at it.

This way of looking at the church is the product of a long story. About the time of the Reformation another movement was brewing. That movement was the Enlightenment. The Enlightenment used the new-found "objective" way of thinking that science uses. Science was a new thing, and it was really working, so people got excited and applied it to all aspects of life. Of course, science has no place for the supernatural, so the "sacred" practices of the church—specifically preaching about a God in human flesh and eating the body and blood of one long dead who was claimed to somehow be alive—were easily declared superstitious and invalid.

When the "sacred" aspects of the church were considered superstitious, only the "secular" aspects were considered valid. The visible church, according to this "scientific" way of thinking, was no different than any other social organization which tries to do good. But to the faithful, this argument never made sense. If you take preaching the Gospel and the sacraments out of the church, there is no church. Those are the only two things that Jesus commanded the visible church to do (because they are the only way God creates and sustains faith in Him). Without them there is no church at all—visible or invisible.

We call these sacred practices, preaching the Gospel and using the sacraments, the "marks" of the church. They are marks for all believers. If people say they are true believers, but they do not hear the Gospel and receive the sacraments, they are fooling themselves. Jesus commissioned His disciples to preach the Good News to all nations and baptize (Matt. 28:19) and to join in the Lord's Supper regularly (1 Cor. 11:25).

You probably understand what the Gospel is (the Good News of Jesus Christ), but you might not know what the sacraments are and what their significance is. The sacraments are visible signs of God's love. They are something you can experience also with your senses rather than merely with your intellect or spirituality, though both of these may be involved. In the sacraments we are touched in body, mind, and spirit by the forgiving love of God. In the Lutheran Church there are two sacraments, Baptism and the Lord's Supper, the two previously mentioned as being commanded by Jesus. In the Roman Catholic Church there are seven sacraments under another definition.

"Teenagers Don't Care"

*T*he fact that the Roman Catholic Church has seven sacraments and the Lutheran Church has only two brings up a difficult issue. If God loves His church, why does He allow it to be so divided? To answer this question we should first be clear about something. The fact that the church is divided does not mean that truth is divided or that God wants the churches to be divided. Nor does the fact that there is one truth necessarily mean that everyone teaches that truth correctly.

I once heard a very prominent youth leader say, "It's a well-known fact that teenagers don't care about doctrine. They're ecumenical." For a while that sounded real good to me—sort of like teenagers are innocent enough to be on the right wavelength. But I don't buy that statement any more. I think teenagers *do* care about doctrine. Teenagers don't just accept everybody's beliefs. They think about them and then make a decision about what they believe. This goes on all the time in my confirmation class.

Teenagers also have the courage to take a stand and affirm what they believe and reject what they don't believe. A good example is your reaction when you are encountered by a pushy cult type who teaches a false understanding of what faith in Christ is all about. Taking a stand against their aggressive approach is hard because often the persuasive techniques of the cult are more developed than the gut reaction of a teenager.

The Cults

*I*f teenagers are so discriminating about what they believe, why do so many of them join cults? This is a complex problem, but let's eliminate one misconception first. The vast majority of people who join cults are young adults, not teenagers. But that is all the more reason for you to consider seriously the seduction of cults.

I remember a deprogrammer who once told me about a young man he had deprogrammed. He said to me, "The deprogramming was a success. We got him out of that satanic cult and into a respectable job pumping gas. If all goes well, he should be getting married and buying his first house pretty soon."

If that is how we measure the value of our lives, then it is no wonder so many young people join cults. If you base your values on material things and status, your life-style is every bit as demonic as that of the "satanic cult," and it is emptier. That is why people join cults. The cults promise to provide meaning, authenticity, and purpose—all those things that will lead you to find your true self. If we base our lives on the ways of the world, they will have so little meaning that anything that promises meaning and authenticity will look good.

Compared to the real thing, cults promise nothing. They have no attraction. But compared to the counterfeit solution, they have little appeal either. That is why cults have little power over people who have totally given up on finding themselves and becoming somebody. People who are totally immersed in the pop culture of our day—a steady diet of video, porn, audio, snacks, cool clothes, drugs, alcohol, sex, movie violence, etc.—are not interested in cults. They have a great one of their own. It is called the "new narcissism" but it is as old as humanity. It is the problem the Israelites were fighting throughout the Old Testament. The problem of idol worship wasn't solely a problem of bowing down to statues. It was a problem of decadent (narcissistic or self-indulgent) behavior. The idol worship was accompanied by riotous orgies, such as when the Israelites made the golden calf.

This discussion about the church has come full circle. Where can you find the "real thing"? You all know places where you do not find community. You all know places where you do not find love and justice, where there is no concern for respecting people or treating people fairly. In societies that encourage material gain and social climbing you will not find community. They are often marked by institutions that encourage extreme individualism and competition. This is often the case in the corporate world and in some schools that claim to prepare students for the "real world." You will not find community where there is manipulating and scheming, where people are always planning to "dog" you or put you down or use you to make themselves look more important or popular. You will not find community where there is a survival mentality and a dog-eat-dog attitude or where the concern for "getting" does away with individual rights, respect, and love. That is exactly where the pop culture, the new narcissism, will lead you. There is nothing inherently evil about video games, rock music, and sex. But when you see video games and hear rock music promoting rape and violence to women, you should recognize the warning signals.

These latter conditions seem subhuman, and indeed they are. They seem like stereotyped ghetto behavior, and if you live in the streets, you know what this means. Have you ever felt like you've been used? like you've been conned? ripped off? violated? Have you ever used someone or ripped someone off? Who doesn't get into the habit of making sure we get what's coming to us—taking care of "number one"? We are this way because we are, like our institutions, fallen. We are locked into grubby materialism, and you know what happens if you don't get smart and fight your way to respect.

This is what we're up against in this world. It is no solution to escape into the new narcissism or a cult. They merely perpetuate the same situation. Nor does it help to take refuge in apocalyptic "endtime" theology. There are a lot of Christian groups waving the red flag of nuclear holocaust and the end of the world. While it is wise to acknowledge that the end could come for you anytime (you could be run over by a truck), it is not right to stop trying to make this a better world. Many of the apocalyptic preachers don't work at all at loving their neighbor *now*—either by providing for their needs or by working for their respect and equal rights. Others are even trying to hasten the end. Some churches, however, are beginning to wave the white flag of peace. In the face of all this nuclear madness, the world has an opportunity for peace. The threat of total destruction is so great that almost everybody wants peace! Don't be fooled by people who see no hope for a peaceful solution.

*T*he New Age

he church has a unique calling among institutions. It is the institution through which God is carrying out His work of reconciling the world to Himself. This means that, in Christ, God accomplished the work that was necessary to get the world back on the right track. Therefore, ever since Jesus rose from the dead, He has been leading His faithful followers, the church, into the New Age, where the reconciliation is complete.

It is exciting to know that as the body of Christ we are participating, each in his or her own way, in bringing in this New Age. We know that as members of His church, we are supposed to love God and love our neighbors, even our enemies, but that is so hard for us to do because we aren't perfect. But God can work with our failures to accomplish His purposes. His Spirit helps us grow in love. As we become older, the Spirit helps us control our impulses and love our neighbor more completely. That does not make us better people, but it increases our enjoyment of life. As a teenager, you have this to look forward to. You can expect to become more and more the person you want to be.

Since we are baptized and believe in Christ, we are already living in the New Age. Jesus told us that the kingdom of God would begin with His resurrection. That means that death is no longer a barrier between the world and heaven. Christians begin their new life from the day they are baptized. This isn't just an empty ritual.

Christians often experience the joy and peace of heaven. This experience is not something for adults only. Children and teenagers experience it also. Maybe you have in a quiet moment outdoors, in a walk with a friend, or in a peaceful talk with a parent.

Still we are human. These experiences of heaven are mingled with experiences of sin and death. From the moment we were born, we were subject to sin and death. That is what we are up against. For a Christian, the situation might appear worse. Not only are we born into sin and death, but we are baptized into the death of Christ. That means we will lead our lives in self-sacrifice like Christ. We might even die for our faith. But don't forget, we were also baptized into the resurrection of Christ, so that sin and death have no power over us, and our sacrifices on the path of Christ's death will be steps of joy along the path in(to) the New Age. The New Age is, and will be, indeed, a new creation. In it we are reborn. In it we become our true selves.

Your Youth Group—A Part of the Church's Total Youth Ministry

A church youth group has a special kind of significance. It is part of your church, and its members who confess Christ are also in the body of Christ. It can be a group that advocates for you, that helps you and other teenagers with the difficult adjustments you have to make during the teen years. If you can deal with your concerns within the context of the church, you can be assured that God will guide you into your true self. You, too, are a child of God, participating in the New Age.

However, do you remember the difference between the visible church and the invisible church? Your youth group is in the "fallen" visible church. As with any other organization, you will have to work at making it a community. You will have to work at helping each other practice love and acceptance. You will have to develop rules and select strong and capable leaders to ensure that respect and fairness are shown toward everyone. Two ground rules we use in our group are confidentiality and clear air space for the one speaking. You will also have to reach out, both within your group and outside it. There is no room for cliques in the kingdom of God. We're all cool in it. The New Age can include anyone, so we will have to look around neighborhoods and schools to find more people to join.

What kinds of activities could a youth group do? It is my opinion that since most of the youth in the group attend worship together on Sundays, it is better to center on activities other than worship. This will give you a chance to experience the presence of God in the fullness of life, in all of Christian fellowship. It will also present a format that will be more inviting for teenagers who are uncertain about their involvement in your particular church or in church in general. You can always invite people to come to worship with you.

Of course, you could make worship one of your activities. One thing that teenagers don't like is boring worship where they feel they are being preached at. You could make it a project to make worship more relevant to teenagers.

One activity that simply cannot be dispensed with is the serious discussion of the important concerns of life, particularly those of the teenage years. Can people talk about important things in your group, or do they always have to joke or be superficial? I have seen many groups go down the tube because they couldn't meet this challenge. It would be wise to ask an adult you trust to lead these discussions. One particularly valuable technique is to break into pairs or triads to talk about a particular concern.

Finally, your church youth group does not have to be the only activity you are in. However, your church is the best center for your life, considering where it is taking you. Your youth group could take on this centering role.

I really hope that you can get a successful youth group going at your church. If things aren't going like you think they should, you can always pray for your group. God always answers the prayers of those who trust in Him. He is interested in your youth group. It too can always start over at any time.

The real joy of participating in your church is experiencing your own growth. As you learn more about yourself and find out who you are, you will begin to reach out and help others with their growth. That is the joy of Christian friendship.

*T*HINGS YOU CAN DO

Individual: Pray for community in your youth group or among people with whom you associate or would like to associate. Investigate the possibility of forming a youth group or of beginning meaningful discussions or service projects in your group.

Group: For this exercise you will want to break into triads—listener, sharer, and observer. Consult the appendix to see how this is done. Take turns sharing. Possible topics are:

1. the thing I would most like to change about myself;
2. the thing that causes me the most conflict; or
3. the event that hurt me the most.

Reconvene in the large group and discuss the experience.

Appendix

Group Exercises

1. *Ground Rules*

In order for your youth group to function in a meaningful way, there must be respect for everybody who comes. In order to guarantee that respect, it is essential to have certain ground rules. You would be happiest if you wrote your own. However, there are two which you absolutely need:

a. *Confidentiality*: Whatever is said in the group stays in the group. All persons must be guaranteed that nothing they say in the group will be told outside of the group. That pertains also to small groups or pairs. Whatever is said in them does not pass without permission into the larger group. Because this ground rule is so important, we request that anyone who violates confidentiality in our group leave the group.

b. *Respect for the speaker*: Whoever is speaking should be allowed to speak without interruption. It is helpful to appoint a trustworthy person as the leader to designate whose turn it is to speak. It is a good idea to work it out so everyone has an opportunity to speak.

There are certainly other rules that could help, such as introducing the group to a newcomer. Be careful not to make too many rules, however.

2. *Roleplaying*

One way to understand your own or someone else's feelings is to roleplay. In roleplaying you pretend you are someone else so you can see yourself or some situation from his or her point of view. In order for roleplaying to work, you must take it seriously. Otherwise it degenerates into the realm of fantasy. That is not to say it cannot contain humor, but don't let the humor slip out of reality.

Roleplaying can be done either in the presence of the whole group or in pairs or triads. When it is done in the presence of the entire group, it is best to do it either in the center of a circle or in front of the entire group. Everyone should have an opportunity to play at least one role and, if time permits, both roles. If roleplaying is done in separate pairs or triads, it will be necessary to have a number of private spaces. If these spaces are not avilable, it is better to roleplay in the group situation so there is not too much noise and distraction.

3. *Peer Counseling*

"Peer counseling" is counseling by people your own age. It works. It is best done in pairs or triads, and, as in roleplaying, it is best to have private spaces for each pair or triad. In pairs one person is a sharer and the other a listener. Prior to pairing off, the entire group can develop a list of specific concerns or problems relating to a specific issue, such as getting along with your parents. Preferably, everyone in the group can contribute an item on the list. Then each person selects either an item from the list or another concern or problem that relates to the issue.

The group members then pair up and move into private rooms or spaces. The adult leaders can participate in this pairing if the group desires. The pairing should either be done by the group leader or by drawing out of a hat; otherwise you might always talk to the same person.

When the pair has settled into its private space, the sharer describes the chosen concern to the listener as completely as possible. Don't leave anything out. The listener listens, interrupting only to encourage the sharer to go on or to ask questions. The listener does not give advice, but tries to encourage the sharer to complete the description of the concern. When the sharer has finished, the listener feeds back what he or she has heard, and the sharer fills in anything that was missed. After the listener has finished, the pair reverses roles. Usually 5—10 minutes is enough for each person, and a timekeeper will have to tell everybody when to switch and when to come back to the group. After each person has completed the exercise, return to the group and tell what happened in your pair. Remember confidentiality! Get permission to tell any confidential details.

In triads an observer is added to the rotation. The observer's task is to watch both the sharer and the listener and to write down body movements and speech characteristics. There should be nothing observed about what is actually said. There are to be no judgments such as, "He looked nervous." You can only observe bodily movements or speech characteristics, such as "She fidgeted in her chair." When the sharing is completed—that is, after the listener has fed back—the observer gives his or her report. Then the observer becomes the listener; the listener, the sharer; and the sharer, the observer for the next round.

There are obviously many more group techniques that may prove to be valuable, and you may develop some novel techniques and approaches. These are some our group has appreciated the most. Good luck!